TODAY

IS THE DAY YOU CHANGE YOUR LIFE

Prentice Hall LIFE

If life is what you make it, then making it better starts here.

What we learn today can change our lives tomorrow. It can change our goals or change our minds; open up new opportunities or simply inspire us to make a difference. That's why we have created a new breed of books that do more to help you make more of *your* life.

Whether you want more confidence or less stress, a new skill or a different perspective, we've designed *Prentice Hall Life* books to help you to make a change for the better. Together with our authors we share a commitment to bring you the brightest ideas and best ways to manage your life, work and wealth.

In these pages we hope you'll find the ideas you need for the life *you* want. Go on, help yourself.

It's what you make it

* * *

TODAY IS THE DAY YOU CHANGE YOUR LIFE

Elaine Harrison

Prentice Hall Life
is an imprint of

Harlow, England • London • New York • Boston • San Francisco • Toronto
Sydney • Tokyo • Singapore • Hong Kong • Seoul • Taipei • New Delhi
Cape Town • Madrid • Mexico City • Amsterdam • Munich • Paris • Milan

PEARSON EDUCATION LIMITED

Edinburgh Gate
Harlow CM20 2JE
Tel: +44 (0)1279 623623
Fax: +44 (0)1279 431059
Website: www.pearson.com/uk

First published in Great Britain in 2011

© Pearson Education Limited 2011

The right of Elaine Harrison to be identified as author of this work has been asserted by her in accordance with the Copyright, Designs and Patents Act 1988.

Pearson Education is not responsible for the content of third-party internet sites.

ISBN: 978-0-273-75040-6

British Library Cataloguing-in-Publication Data
A catalogue record for this book is available from the British Library

Library of Congress Cataloging-in-Publication Data
Harrison, Elaine, 1963–
    Today is the day you change your life / Elaine Harrison.
        p. cm.
    ISBN 978-0-273-75040-6 (pbk.)
    1. Change (Psychology) 2. Self-realization. I. Title.
    BF637.C4H365 2011
    158--dc22

                                        2011014896

10 9 8 7 6 5 4 3 2 1
15 14 13 12 11

Design by Design Deluxe
Typeset in 11pt Minion Pro by 3
Printed and bound in Great Britain by Ashford Colour Press Ltd, Gosport, Hampshire

CONTENTS

ACKNOWLEDGEMENTS

For me, writing this book has been a journey – with many changes along the way! – and therefore I would like to acknowledge those I met on the path.

The ones who were there when the journey was just an idea: Andrew McFarlane and the LeadChange team, thankyou for inspiration, opportunity and fun. Perry, thankyou for your secretarial skills, your belief in my ideas and your boys' trips to buy me time. Sandra Sedgbeer (a master of change), thankyou for forever friendship, belief in my writing and inspiration – from near or afar.

And those who stayed with me throughout: Mum, Dad, Steven, Fiona, Peter, Gillian, James, Sarah and Sophie – the greatest back-up team ever! Thankyou is too small a word.

To Terry, Jim and your gorgeous children – thankyou for your ever-welcoming hearth and the laughter when most needed.

To those who waved the green flag for go: Caroline Jordan (wherever you are), thankyou for placing my book idea in just the right hands. Rachael Stock from Pearson, immense thanks for your leap of faith, wonderful feedback and making it all happen. To all the Production, Sales and Marketing folk who have placed this book in your hands.

And last, but by no means least: to Joseph for being a catalyst for change and a motivator. And Archie, for being such a shining shadow and great foot-warmer.

INTRODUCTION

The idea of changing your life can seem daunting when you look at everything at once. I want a new job, a better relationship, to get fit, to lose weight, to move home, to reduce my stress levels… Oh, and I want it now. Whoah! When you start to list all the things you might like to change, it can feel pretty overwhelming. Add a sense of urgency and it feels even worse. So most of us give up before we get started. Or decide to wait. Wait until next week, until next month, until we are feeling happier, until someone else 'does something', until we feel more motivated, until…

How do we stop it all feeling overwhelming? I once had a very large jar that I put my small change into, just a few coins a few times a week. The first few times I put some money in it felt odd – not something I was 'used' to doing – and I did have to remind myself on a couple of occasions. After a while it became a familiar habit. Then one day – I have no recollection of how long it took – the jar was full, to the tune of almost £250! Life change is like that too, a little bit here and there soon adds up… It needn't be stressful and, best of all, you needn't wait any longer. You really can start today.

Change comes in many guises. There are moments in life when things happen and you find yourself profoundly changed forever. There are also periods where nothing much seems to happen at all. But there is one certainty in life – things will change. Seasons change, the weather changes, people change, jobs change, technology changes, relationships change, opinions change, you change… resisting change is futile. Digging your heels in and trying to stop change happening isn't good for you, or for anybody around you. You get the best from life by letting it happen, going with it, making the most of it, initiating change even, however scary it might feel at first.

There are millions of people around the world at any time who are looking for change. How do you know if you're one of them? The need for change can be spotted in a number of ways, from a niggling sense of restlessness to a nagging dissatisfaction, from an underlying irritability to a daily despondency as you drag yourself out of bed for another day in the life of you. The desire for change can manifest as anger, depression, constant daydreaming, procrastination, or the realisation that you had some dreams and goals years ago and you're no nearer reaching them today than you were then.

It's time to take action. I want you to imagine for a moment that you have complete control over your life; that you even have control over your past (at least your thoughts about it!) and over your future. Imagine that you can change your life right now, right here, right away! With no need for major financial investment, years of study, mystical intervention – you can change your life for the better, right now. How good does that sound? Well, it's true. You can.

It's time to stop waiting for anyone else to do it for you, or for anyone else to change to make things better in your world. Change is an inside job. Sometimes people seemingly are handed amazing life changes on a plate: they win lotteries, are offered amazing opportunities, get lucky! But months down the line (money squandered, opportunities wasted and luck run out) they are back to square one. External changes don't really make much of a long-term difference unless accompanied or pre-empted by internal changes. Sometimes these have to come first, and sometimes they will come a little way down the line – in other words, you may have to act first and change later.

There's a truth that most people do not like: whatever you're getting is caused by whatever you're doing. But it is a truth that carries immense power – do something different and you'll get something different. Be different and you will see different results. You don't have to trek halfway around the world to search for some kind of magic – you have it within you, you are it, YOU are the one who can change your life, starting right now if you so wish. In fact you have taken the first step already – you've started reading this book and in doing so have taken the first action towards making life better for you.

This book is about figuring out what you want (and what you don't want), about deciding where you're heading and how to get there. It will guide you through a process of discovery and empower you to get back into the driving seat of your life. You will learn how to write a 'pro-active goals' list, and discover how it can change your life in remarkable and upbeat ways. You will learn how to make peace with your past and muster all your resources – your mind-chatter, intuition, imagination and well-being – to create an unstoppable winning force.

This book is about change and, though it will ask you to create goals and visions for the future, it's also about making changes NOW, taking those first all-important steps and discovering for yourself how small changes can make big differences. Throughout you will find a down-to-earth, no-nonsense, no-mysticism-required approach to living the life you desire. Whether you are seeking major or minor changes, the principles remain the same – do something different and you will get a different result.

Putting off change in your life will keep you stuck in the waiting room, wondering and worrying about what will happen when you leave its safe confines. Worrying is using your imagination to create something you don't want. Wondering… now that might just get you somewhere, but only if you act upon it! It's all about the doing.

I am going to ask you to write things down as you journey through this book, so you may want to get yourself a special 'Life Changes' notebook, something you can keep by you for whenever you want to revisit what you've already written, or add to as ideas and thoughts occur. I suggest you keep this notebook confidential – or only share it with someone you trust: a special someone who supports you unconditionally in your desire to change and grow; someone with no agenda other than to encourage you.

Life is too short to be spent doing things you don't want to do, spending time with people you don't want to be with, having dreams and ambitions you never pursue, worrying… the list goes on. This is no dress rehearsal, this is it! Don't waste this lifetime.

When you're healthy (ish) and life seems to be rolling along OK (ish), when the waves you're riding aren't too big (ish) and the traumas are not too great (ish), it's easy to be lulled into a false sense of being OK (ish) – especially if you keep busy enough not to think about any alternatives, or douse any signs of discontent with the odd glass of wine/beer/cigarette/chocolate/ manic workout/feverish stint of cleaning. But do you ever sense a small voice inside that wishes life were different? Or even a big voice? Of course you do! That's why you're reading this book.

Now, before you start listening to that other voice that says 'Oh, we're just fine the way we are, there's no point changing things and chasing after dreams because it will only end in tears', score yourself from 1–10 against each of the following statements, where 1 equals 'this is not true at all' and 10 equals 'this is absolutely true 100 per cent of the time':

1–10
(1 = not true at all; 10 = true 100% of the time)

I am in the perfect relationship for me   _____

I am doing work that I love   _____

I am always true to myself   _____

I am pursuing my dreams and ambitions   _____

I am happy with 'my lot'   _____

Any scores below 10? Then there is room for improvement – it is time to make some changes. You deserve it!

Humans are creatures of habit. Routines and rituals help to give some structure and familiarity to life. We get used to things, even painful things, and they become normal. And of course if these things are taken away from us, or change is forced upon us, we don't like it. If you had a pain in your tooth for years and finally had it removed you would feel better, but you would miss it, too, because it was familiar and you lived life accordingly. Why wait so long? And why wait until change is forced upon you? This is your life and, as much as you might find it difficult to accept, it is all the way it is because of your thoughts and choices. Different thoughts and choices = a different life.

The very fact that you have this book in your hands means you have already taken the first step towards changing your life. You can start the process of change right now, by doing something different, taking a first step, or changing your thinking. Throughout the book you will find 'Things to do today', things that may only take the five minutes you have to spare – but will make big differences.

You can change your life, starting right now. Today. Even the longest and most arduous journeys begin with just one step – and taken step by step they are not so long or so arduous. If you could see your ideal world/relationship/home/job/life at the end of a dark tunnel, if you could be sure it was there and waiting for you, certain that it would be all you ever dreamed of (maybe even more!), that you could be happier and more fulfilled than you ever thought possible, would you venture into the tunnel? Would you brave the journey? Could you step into what appears to be a dark and scary place for a while?

Let me come with you while you peek into that tunnel. I'll even walk through it with you if you like. Keep this book close by and know that you are never alone on your journey. And remember, the tunnel may not be scary at all; it may be shorter than you think and even fun! Believe me, it feels amazingly good to start tackling things and making changes. It's liberating, uplifting and life-enhancing to find yourself back in charge. So let's go!

1

TODAY IS THE DAY YOU KNOW WHERE YOU'RE STARTING FROM

What do you feel are the major 'problem' areas in your life right now? Do you want a better job or relationship? Are you fed up with where and how you live? Tired of feeling the way you do? Do you long for something – but are not sure what it is? Or would you rather just exchange the whole lot and get a new, improved life?

Whatever you want, you've got to start 'where you are' and that means taking a good honest look at how you feel about your life right now. Awareness of how things are is a great motivator for change. It can also help you highlight the 'biggie' – the one thing that is affecting all the other areas of your life, the one that will have roll-on repercussions the minute you begin to address it.

Awareness is a great motivator for change

Review your life

Here's an opportunity to rate yourself and your life in a number of areas. It is helpful to write your answers down and to go with your initial gut response. Be honest – this is for you – nudging the scores up to make them look better won't really help at all. Score yourself from 1–10 against each of the following statements, where 1 equals 'this is not true at all' and 10 equals 'this is absolutely true 100 per cent of the time'.

Before you start I had better warn you, this kind of honest review can seriously change your life – for the better! However, it is not always easy to look at how you feel about things and rate them, and the list below is by no means exhaustive. For instance, you may feel there are many things that are perfect about your relationship, but want to change certain aspects of it – so you may stall at the first item. That's OK, just acknowledge what it is 'along that theme' you wish to change and score accordingly. You may also feel different about things on different days – that's OK too. If there are days when you feel 'I am in control of my finances' and days when you feel 'I am so out of control of my finances' you could rate yourself twice – for the good days and the bad (though the reality is your 'true' score will probably lie somewhere between the two). There may also be some areas that do not apply to you. This is just a starting point, an opportunity to review your life as it is today. You can of course grab a pen and add to and delete from the list, making it more appropriate and personal for you. If you find yourself stuck on any item just move onto the next – you may wish to come back to it later.

I also want you to take note if you find the very suggestion that anyone might score 10 against any of these things a little outrageous, silly, irresponsible, or unrealistic. If you do I suggest you mark them with a large asterix, exclamation mark or similar and come back to them later – a few chapters later maybe – when your life is changing and so are your expectations.

1–10
(1 = not true at all; 10 = true 100% of the time)

I am in the perfect relationship for me	_____
I trust that the perfect relationship is on its way	_____
I am doing work that I love	_____
I am on the perfect career path for me	_____
I get excited about going to work	_____
I am always true to myself	_____
I know what I want	_____
I am clear about my goals, dreams and ambitions	_____
I am pursuing my goals, dreams and ambitions	_____
I am physically healthy	_____
I feel mentally sharp and alert	_____

▶

I love my body   _____

I enjoy regular exercise   _____

I enjoy holidays and time-out to recharge myself   _____

I am in control of my finances   _____

I eat nourishing, health-giving foods   _____

I am free of addictions   _____

I have a great and supportive social circle   _____

I regularly find time to do things I enjoy   _____

I always imagine the best possible outcomes   _____

I feel mentally and emotionally balanced   _____

I have a great relationship with my parents   _____

I spend quality time with my children   _____

My home is my sanctuary   _____

I sleep well and wake refreshed every morning   _____

I have a sense of 'purpose' in life   _____

My role in the world is an important one   _____

I have faith in a power greater than myself   _____

I am happy with 'my lot'   _____

I am at peace with my past   _____

This inventory is your own personal reference point; it is designed to help you see where you are at now. It is a way of bringing out feelings you would maybe rather ignore and in some instances your scores may surprise you. They may certainly surprise other people but I suggest you either keep them confidential or only share them with people you trust and who unconditionally support you on your journey.

 THINGS TO DO TODAY: Complete the full inventory if you can. If you can't, just do whatever you have time for – rating even just one area of your life; you can always complete the rest later. Even doing it one line at a time will be a step forward. Just do what you can, when you can.

Know yourself

Your scores will have already given you a clear picture of areas in your life where there is room for improvement. Some of them – regardless of the number given – may carry a greater emotional charge than others. For instance a 3 for 'I sleep well and wake refreshed every morning' may prompt a knowing nod and a realisation that sleep is an area requiring some focus (indeed that alone could nudge other scores upwards!), but a 3 against 'I am in the perfect relationship for me' could create a stomach-churning mixture of emotions.

 THINGS TO DO TODAY: Rate your whole life on a scale of 1–10 (where 1 equals 'nothing is working the way I want it to' and 10 equals 'life is just perfect'). Now see what you can do today to nudge that score up a point, and maybe one point more?

Be gentle with yourself. If any areas have surprised you, know that all you are doing is bringing to the surface things you already knew deep down. Repression and depression sound similar for good reasons – if you keep on ignoring and repressing feelings they don't go away, they just get de-pressed back down

Know that all you are doing is bringing to the surface things you already knew deep down

and resurface in other guises until you just have to pay attention. The greatest gift you can give yourself is to listen to yourself and start to make changes before change is forced upon you. And if you feel the need to sigh and say 'But I can't be so self-centred – I've got people who rely on me and they come first', then remember what they say during the safety talk on aeroplanes: 'in an emergency parents with children should put their own oxygen masks on before assisting their children' – otherwise they just might not be able to help them at all!

What to do next

So now you have a list of figures alongside a list of statements about your life – a clear indicator of 'where you are at right now'. What do you think would happen if you did nothing different? If you just kept doing what you're doing, repeating the same patterns of behaviour and playing the same roles? I suggest one of three things might happen:

1 Nothing would change.

2 Things could get worse!

or

3 You would now be unable to resist change for the better – because sometimes awareness by itself is curative.

And what do you think might happen if you started doing things differently – in a positive way that suits you best? Here the possibilities are endless, but a few might be:

1 You could start to feel better right away – right now.

2 Things would just get better and better, day by day.

3 Life would take on a new air of excitement and possibility.

4 You could start to feel more alive than ever before.

5 At long last – you'd be back in the driving seat of your life.

6 Things might go through a slightly uncomfortable period as you – and others – adapt to change. Be prepared for this possibility and know it will pass.

Future you's

Let's take two scenarios. First, I want you to imagine yourself in 20 years' time if you remain on your current life course and do nothing different. Imagine that things just stay the same (or maybe even get worse) for the next 20 years. How do you imagine you will look? What will it feel like being that future you? What might you be doing? What will your health and vitality be like? Where will you be? Who with? Where will you be on a happiness scale of 1–10 (where 1 equals miserable and 10 equals very happy)?

Now I want you to imagine yourself in 20 years' time after making many positive changes in your life. Imagine that you read your life review in this book and committed to take action to turn your life around for the better. Imagine you succeeded in everything you wanted to do. How do you imagine this future you will look? How will you feel? What will you be doing? How healthy and energetic will you be? Where will you be? Who else will be with you? Where will you be on a happiness scale of 1–10?

I want you to really bring these two possible future you's alive in your imagination. Maybe even give them names. And I want you to use them to spur you on when you need a helping hand. When you are faced with choices – from what to eat for dinner to what career path to choose – check in with these two and see what choices they would have made. What advice can they give you? Who are you going to listen to?

A friend whose life was heading on a collision course to disaster tried this exercise and the names she gave her two possible future selves were self-explanatory: Mrs Dead and Mrs Alive. As she faced another possible weekend of binge drinking she checked in with the two of them and thankfully took the advice of the latter. She now describes herself as: 'more alive than I have ever felt before.'

 THINGS TO DO TODAY: Put a time in your diary to complete the future you's exercise. Or even just start to think about it when you have a moment to yourself – maybe on a short journey.

2
TODAY IS THE DAY YOU KNOW WHAT YOU *DON'T* WANT

Your intention to make changes is there because something, or things, in your life are not OK for you any more – or maybe they have never been. Intention is a powerful force and it is yours to use at any time. The world can be crashing down around your ears, but how you react is not dependent on circumstances: it is in your control (trust me on this – you may not be feeling that way right now!). Unfortunately in our often busy and chaotic lives we can lose sight of this and instead fall victim to circumstances – ricocheting from one seeming misfortune to another. If that sounds like you, then congratulations, because in your hands you now have a life raft and between us we are going to steer it to wherever you want to go. And one step towards that is determining where you do *not* want to go.

 THINGS TO DO TODAY: Stop right now and check in with yourself. What is there about today that you don't want? What can you do to change it? What different choice/s could you make? If the change seems too big, how can you break it down into small chunks? How can you make a 5, 10 or 20 per cent change?

Let me start with a metaphor. Imagine your life is a house, complete with all its rooms, furniture, fixtures and fittings, cupboards, drawers and shelves full of 'stuff', its hidden corners, its décor, and maybe even outbuildings, a garage and a garden – or more. Now imagine you want to change that house; you no longer feel at home and OK there because it just doesn't look and feel right any more (maybe it never did). Maybe you want to redecorate, reorganise and rearrange what you already have, or perhaps you would like to throw out a lot of your old possessions and bring in some completely new things, or even up sticks and move somewhere else. Where do you start?

One option would be to decorate over the top of the existing paint or paper, move a few things around or buy something new

Papering over the cracks is rarely a good solution

and add it to the mix. Another would be to sell up and move on. In both instances, unless you take a good honest look at what you have already got, decide what you no longer want or need, be sure about what works and what doesn't work for you, you could well end up feeling just as dissatisfied. Papering over the cracks is rarely a good solution; neither is continually buying new stuff when you haven't sorted out what you already have. And radical measures, such as moving all your baggage halfway round the world is not – on its own – going to get you the house (or life) of your dreams.

Sometimes it is difficult to pinpoint exactly what you do want. When your life is filled with things you don't want, it can be difficult to see beyond them. And sometimes it is difficult to be sure exactly what you don't want, because we just get used to things and never question if they're OK for us any more. We just don't know! If this is a familiar conundrum for you I suggest you start with a spring clean.

Spring cleaning

OK, it's time to clear through all the old rubbish, all the stuff you're done with, the stuff you've inherited but never really wanted, the baggage you're tired of carrying and the burdens that wear you down. It's time to spring clean your life!

One of the easiest ways to get things going is to create a 'Things I Do Not Want' list. Write down all the things that you no longer want in your life. Get a piece of paper (or two!) and let rip. These may be situations, events, objects – maybe even people... and that's fine. Get it all off your chest and out of your head and onto the paper. You may find it helpful if you use what is sometimes called 'stream of consciousness' writing – in other words you just write whatever comes into your mind and let the words flow, unedited. Don't worry about spelling or grammar – or even 'sense' at this point. Just use this opportunity to be searingly honest about what you no longer want. Keep writing even if you feel stuck; if the words seem to be drying up just scribble 'blah, blah, blah,' until you can start again. Don't start to censor what you've written at this point – just let's see what emerges.

Write out all the things that you find annoying, frustrating and painful, the things that are in your way and contribute to you feeling unfulfilled and unsatisfied, the things you are fed up with and the things you want to change. The writing down is important – it can be cathartic. Remember, every action in life is preceded by a thought, but often our thoughts are not clear or we are not fully conscious of them. Writing them down can help you become aware of your thoughts, to crystallise them and better understand them. Only then can you be truly motivated to take the kind of action required for positive change.

IMAGINE A CHANGE

If you are unable to start your full 'Do Not Want' pages right now, start by thinking of just one thing that is going to be on your list. Be really clear in your mind what it is and what you are going to write. Once you are clear, I want you to turn it around by stating what you do want instead. Again, be really clear and as specific as you can. Now turn it into a mantra, starting with the words: 'I am . . .'. State what you do want as if you already have it, for example, 'I don't want this job. I do want a new job', becomes: 'I am doing work I love'. Repeat it to yourself throughout the day. Make it as real as possible. By doing this one quick, simple exercise you have started a chain of reactions. You have already made a change. And for just one thing it can be done on the shortest of journeys or in the five spare minutes you have when waiting for someone.

Sometimes it can help to put headings on your paper to concentrate your mind on specific areas, such as work, relationships, health, social life, finances... and so on. It's OK if your page or pages look messy and disorganised – no one else is going to read them. Write and rant till you are all done... till you have got it all out. Nothing is too petty or too big for your 'Do Not Want' pages.

Once you know what you no longer want, you are one HUGE step closer to knowing what you do want – and what you need to change in order to get it. Getting rid of old stuff also leaves space for the new.

For some people, even identifying what they do not want is difficult and there can be many reasons for this. If this applies to you, here's another approach: take a pen and paper and simply state how things are right now – without judging or labelling them as 'good' or 'bad', as 'things you do not want' or 'things to change'. Just be honest and review where you are at now, what is actually happening day to day, week to week. Use headings if it helps you to focus: work, relationships, family, health, finances, social life... and so on.

> Work is causing me great stress.
>
> I am worried about bills and money much of the time.
>
> My relationship is not going well, we are not communicating much.
>
> There is no quality time with the children.
>
> I am enjoying going to the gym.

Take a good honest look at your present situation – when things are brought out into the open and looked at, your feelings about them will surface and motivate you to make changes.

Turnaround time

Identifying what you no longer want in your life is a very positive motivator for change. But it is no good stopping there. Focusing on what you do not want is a stepping stone to a better place – it is not a place to dwell. There is a saying 'You get what you focus on' – and it is true!

Whatever your age, you have a certain number of years of life experience. If you have accumulated negative feelings about those experiences you will probably see life negatively, and your way of seeing life will colour everything you do. Likewise, if you have accumulated positive feelings about life your actions and reactions will reflect this. Our experiences create our beliefs about the world. The pictures you make in your imagination and the way you talk to yourself (your internal chatter) is based upon your own personal experiences and beliefs about life – not on reality – and your life will reflect these. That is why we always get more of what we focus on in our life.

 THINGS TO DO TODAY: Choose your thoughts wisely. If you focus on what you don't want you might just get more of it! Focus instead on what you do want.

A classic example was the snowfall of 2010. I love snow! It reminds me of skiing trips, sledging expeditions, the fun of snowman building, the laughter and excitement of snowball fights, the thrill of creating ice-slides and the sheer picture-perfectness of a snow-covered landscape. Oh, and then there is the roaring log fire, the hot mugs of soup... you get the picture.

Now a friend of mine (while admitting to having enjoyed fun in the snow on occasions) sees snow as a cold and miserable hindrance to his work outside with horses. It reminds him of freezing pipes, slipping and sliding with buckets of water across fields, machinery not starting, and hurting with cold.

So when the snow came the pictures and thoughts that ran through our minds as a result of the same snowy scene were quite different – as were our moods and consequently our experiences.

We get more of what we focus on

We get more of what we focus on – be it negative or positive. So focusing on a 'Do Not Want' list is not a great idea – unless you wish to create more of the same! To start with I want you to shift your focus right now by changing the title at the top of your list to: 'Things I Am Going to Change'.

Now let's shift the focus onto what you *do* want, prompted by what we've established you *don't* want. For every item on your list of things you are going to change, I want you to 'turn it around' and state what you 'Do Want' instead, using the words 'My goal is to...'. Here are a few examples to help you along:

Do Not Wants	Possible Turnarounds
I do not want to stay in this job	My goal is to find another job.
	My goal is to be a...
	My goal is to start my own business.
	My goal is to go back to college and re-study.
I do not want to argue continually with my partner.	My goal is to get relationship counselling.
	My goal is to leave my partner.
	My goal is to find the perfect relationship for me.

Do Not Wants	Possible Turnarounds
	My goal is to change my behaviour.
I do not want to be overweight.	My goal is to be slimmer.
	My goal is to be fitter.
	My goal is to feel better about myself.
	My goal is to be a size...

Be sure to make your turnaround statement a positive one. For instance, if one of the things you are going to change is 'being overweight', you may be tempted to turn that around to something like 'My goal is to stop eating fattening foods'. Do you see how that still leaves you with another 'do not want'? An alternative would be 'My goal is to eat healthy, nutritious foods', and/or 'My goal is to take regular exercise and get fitter'.

Now you have something to aim towards, something positive to focus on. You have given your brain a 'tracking device' and it will begin to help you find what you do want – rather than keeping you spinning in a maelstrom of things you don't want. Sometimes it is as easy as that! If you know what you do want you can start making different choices right now and your life will begin to change. Keep doing the same things and you will keep getting the same results. Different choices equals a different life.

A QUICK CHANGE

During a coaching session a client of mine recognised how he often focused on what he did not want – and how that kept getting him more of the same. At the end of the session I suggested he may like to do the list exercise above as a step to discovering what he really did want. Fired with enthusiasm he borrowed a pen and pad to get started during his commute home.

The next time we met he was quite different. He explained how he had felt unable to write his list on the way home; the tube was packed and he couldn't concentrate. Instead he decided to sit back, close his eyes and think about what would be on his list. Top of his list was something he expected to face that very evening. He did not want to go home and be nagged again by his wife for wanting to sit in front of the TV for half an hour, rather than talk through their respective days as soon as he got through the door. He described how even thinking about the usual scenario caused him to bristle with irritation.

His turnaround was: 'I want to enjoy a relaxing half hour in front of the TV and then enjoy talking to my wife'. He allowed his imagination to create the perfect scenario for him and the more he did this the more he relaxed – so much so that he fell asleep! Refreshed and relaxed he enjoyed the short stroll from station to home and for the first time he could remember he entered his home feeling peaceful and calm at the end of a long day.

And this is where, in his words, 'the magic began'. He went on to describe how the exact scenario he had imagined during the train journey unfolded before his very eyes. His wife was happy to see him, there were no cross words, he sat and relaxed in front of the TV for half an hour and then over dinner they talked happily about their days.

▶

Imagining what he did want had altered his state to such an extent that his wife reacted to him quite differently. Rather than being faced with a tense and anxious husband who apparently wanted to ignore her for half an hour, she was met by a relaxed and calm man who needed a bit of time to himself before enjoying dinner and a chat. Magic!

People pleasing

If you take your age and subtract 2, that is how many years you have spent learning to please others. It is our nature. From a very young age we learn to do things that please our parents, grandparents, family and friends. We seek praise, acknowledgement and approval – we want to fit in! And to a degree that's fine and plays a part in creating a stable and cooperative society. However, as the trend continues through school, university, work and relationships, it is possible to lose sight of what we really want, as opposed to what we do to please everyone else. You may well find that your 'Do Not Want' list included things you have taken on board in order to fit in and please others.

BEING TRUE TO YOURSELF

As a child John learnt that the best way to get heaps of praise and love was to say nice things to his parents – it distracted them from their preoccupation with computers, work and TV and got him lots of hugs. When he started school he applied the same tactic to friends and sometimes they laughed at him, so he copied them instead and started calling the other children silly names – this worked because it made everyone laugh! By senior school he had perfected the art of

▶

playing the clown, only now it got him into trouble and he got angry and frustrated. He tried a few relationships, seeking that same praise and love he sought from his parents, and it seemed to work – if he just went along with what the other wanted and kept saying nice things they liked him. Work provided new challenges and again the best tactic seemed to be to just agree with the boss – he liked John, he got promoted... life was good. Or was it?

Actually, no it wasn't. John had lost himself in his constant preoccupation with people-pleasing. He no longer knew what he really wanted for himself; he was so caught up in fitting in and described himself as 'generally unhappy'. Thankfully John realised he wanted his life to change and he began by identifying what he no longer wanted. He discovered what he did want. He also started being authentic and true to himself, always kind and thoughtful, but no longer a people-pleaser to the detriment of his own well-being. John is now happily married and doing work he loves. And without even trying, he has found himself a wonderful circle of friends who love him just the way he is.

Putting yourself first

Time and time again many clients get uncomfortable at the thought of putting themselves first. And time and time again I remind them to take a balanced view and tune-in to their own personal 'who to help' radar. Of course there are times when others' needs take priority (a sick child, frail relative, troubled partner), and no one requires telling when this is the case as it is usually plainly obvious and non-negotiable. However, unless we look after ourselves we are not fully able to be of optimum help to others. So even in times when we choose to put others first, they benefit most if we also find a way to look after ourselves – even in small doses. If you are a 'yes' person – someone whom everyone relies upon to do whatever needs doing, someone who always says 'yes' when asked for help – have a go at breaking the mould. Next time someone calls upon you to do something that is going to require your time and effort say, 'I am not sure'. Tell them you will check your diary and get back to them with an answer 'tomorrow' (or even the next day). Give yourself time to reflect on whether you really do have, and are willing to give, the time and energy – and prepare them for a possible 'no'.

 THINGS TO DO TODAY: Identify any area of your life where you are seeking to fit in, where you are putting others before yourself in order to be liked/seek approval/keep the peace. Ask yourself, if you could be guaranteed a successful outcome, what would you do differently? How could you begin to make a change towards being more authentic today? What small step could you take? What could you say 'no' to? And what could you say 'yes' to? Being true to yourself is one of the greatest gifts you can give yourself – and others!

Being true to yourself is one of the greatest gifts you can give yourself – and others!

3

TODAY IS
THE DAY
YOU DECIDE
WHAT YOU
DO WANT

So, you know you want things to be different. You know that life as it is doesn't quite come up to the mark. But are you really clear yet about all that you DO want? About exactly how you would like your life to be? Hopefully by now you'll be a lot clearer on what you *don't* want, and that's a great start, but trying to act only on the basis of what you don't want is rather like heading off on a journey without knowing where you want to go – helpful only to a point! I'll bet that if you got into the passenger seat of a car and told the driver where you didn't want to go you'd not get very far, and what's more you'd probably end up arguing too. Or imagine heading off to the supermarket with a list of what you don't want to buy!

Research into people who are living their dreams shows that one of the things these happy people have in common is they all knew what they wanted. Their visions were unwavering, though never set in stone – because another common theme is their ability to be flexible and open to new possibilities. Sometimes the simple act of deciding what you do want sets a magical chain of actions into motion and before you know it you are there – doing/being/having whatever it was you wanted. Mind you, this magical process should also carry a warning, which is '*be careful what you wish for*'.

> **Sometimes the simple act of deciding what you want sets a magical chain of actions into motion**

WHEN WISHES COME TRUE

A farmer friend of mine was feeling thoroughly fed-up with looking after his huge herd of cows. He wished he didn't have to have so many to look after. He wished it so much that one day he didn't pay attention when leaving the field and forgot to latch the gate correctly. That very evening his wish came true (albeit for a short

▶

space of time) – there were no cows left in his field! Thankfully there was a happy ending. All the cows were found unharmed and returned with minimal fuss to their pasture. And my farmer friend decided it was time to think about what he really wanted – he is now a carpenter friend.

For most people, however, reaching their chosen destination in life is less of a magical process and more of a practical step-by-step one (though it is worth reiterating that it can often seem like magic is at work once you have a clear picture of what you really want). And with advancements in Quantum Physics, it is becoming increasingly evident that life does have what would have once been perceived as magical qualities. There is now plenty to prove the influence of the mind over the body – and with 'the mind' now being measurable without even touching the head, it would seem that thoughts do not only inhabit the confines of our bodies. How is it that you sometimes know who is on the other end of the phone before you answer it (even before it rings!), and what is it that sometimes prompts you to take a detour or alter your plans only to discover later it was a very wise move?

 THINGS TO DO TODAY: Put your mind to work for you right now. What do you want to feel at this moment? Is there an ache, pain or some tension in your body? Are you feeling stressed, worried, anxious or unsure about something? Close your eyes, take a couple of deep breaths and focus your thoughts on the feeling in your body or mind that you wish to change. Focus on relaxing the thought or feeling, warming it, cooling it, caring for it... whatever feels appropriate.

Allow me to let you into a secret: there is a little bit of you (well, in most people anyway) that doesn't want to change. However uncomfortable it may be, the 'familiar' can feel oddly comfortable. Well, the great news is we can help that little bit of you to feel safe and ease it into changes that may at the moment seem scary. Change does not have to involve leaping off the edge of a cliff (metaphorically speaking), even the largest changes occur in tiny increments – and in many instances tiny changes are all that are required to make massive differences in life. And they can happen right now!

Change something by even the smallest percentage and your outcomes will be different

If you were about to launch a rocket into space – headed for the moon – and at the last minute you changed the trajectory by a tiny fraction, you'd end up some place else. And life is like that. Change something by even the smallest percentage and your outcomes will be different. Change something, anything, now and your life will begin to change.

DO SOMETHING DIFFERENT

Life is often a series of habits and routines – things we always do – which is fine if those habits and routines are creating the life you really desire. If not, then you need to do something different. Start small – in any area of life – and, like dropping even the tiniest pebble in water, there will be ripples. Here are some suggestions to get you started (think of some of your own, too):

Take a different route to work/school/the shops.

Eat something different for breakfast.

Have a no-TV day.

▶

Do five minutes stretching/yoga when you get out of bed.

Wear something different.

Go somewhere you've never been before.

Talk to somebody you've never spoken to before.

Fill three pages with unedited thoughts.

Let's get started

What do you really want?

I know the very question can cause many of us simply to freeze with indecision, but what you say now doesn't have to be your final answer – no one is going to hold you to it – it's just a way to get your 'change muscle' flexing and ready for action. See it as a practice if you like. Come on, nothing is too big, or too small – what do you *really* want? Let's have an unfiltered, uncensored, untampered-with response; forget for a moment all the 'buts' and 'what ifs'. Take a deep breath, relax and calmly and clearly ask yourself the following question:

'What do I *really* want?'

Now close your eyes and just allow the answer/s to pop into your head – it may come as a picture, a word, a feeling or a sound. It may be LOUD and clear, or quiet and unclear, it may be lingering or fleeting, it may be a long list or a one-liner and… it may not be there at all. If it does come – write it down.

Learn to listen to yourself

You might not have listened to yourself properly for a long time. Maybe you've been too busy to take any notice of feelings about things bubbling under the surface. Treat the part of you that knows the answer like a young vulnerable child who is afraid to speak, or is unaccustomed to being asked for answers. Hassling, getting frustrated, being annoyed and nagging won't work. If you tense up and get cross, there will be no answers. However, if you're reassuring, remain calm, open, and simply 'be there' ready to listen whenever he or she is ready to talk – then those answers will come.

Imagine for a moment that the part of you that knows the answer is separate from you. Are they used to being heard? Or have they been ignored for a long time? Are they more accustomed to being told to hush and put others first? Or have they been laughed at or ridiculed for their wants in the past? Be patient, you may need to re-find your 'inner voice' and, like an unused muscle, get it back into shape. As with a child who's afraid to speak, you may need to just show them you are listening and interested, ready to hear when they are ready to speak – then they will surprise you and come out with something very detailed. Be encouraging and attentive – to yourself!

Take notice of things that may draw your attention once you start exploring what you really want. A part of you has heard the question and is ready and working on the answer, or answers. You may suddenly find yourself drawn to a page in a book, magazine or newspaper, a small sign in a shop window or a massive billboard. Or maybe you will hear something on the radio, see something on the TV or overhear a conversation. If something suddenly draws your attention – pay attention. I remember asking myself a 'what do I want?' question some time ago and feeling a little despondent with an apparent lack of response. But life was busy and my 'head' was full – little room for anything it seemed. Then as I walked past a bookshop on my way home I felt compelled to go and have a quick peek along the shelves – I had a whole five minutes to spare. Among hundreds of books my focus went to just one – the very one that prompted the answer to my question! It took less than five minutes to make a life change.

Ask yourself questions

And you can ask different questions too. Or ask the same question many times each day. (Repeating a question throughout the day is fine as long as you feel relaxed about it; it is not fine if you feel nagged and hassled.) Whatever suits you best. Other questions might be:

'What do I want to change about my life right now?'

'What can I do today to improve my life?'

'What would make me happy?'

'What do I want more of?'

'What do I want less of?'

'What do I need for me right now?'

'What would I do if I were guaranteed success?'

'What is best for me?'

Ask yourself when you are in the car, or walking from A to B. Just see what happens. Ask yourself before you go to bed and see how you feel in the morning. Write your chosen question or questions out on post-it notes and stick them around the home/office as reminders.

 THINGS TO DO TODAY: Imagine you are 90 years old (or more) and you are looking back over your life. Is there anything you wish you had done? Is there anything you regret not being or having? What would you most like people to remember you for?

REMEMBER: The answer/s to your question or questions may come in small increments, or from unexpected sources – they may not be 'eureka' moments.

If you are unaccustomed to asking yourself questions you can practise checking in and asking yourself things through the day. For many people deciding what they really want is a process of re-discovery – after years of doing what other people want you to do and putting yourself anyplace but first you simply may not know anymore. So practise by asking yourself questions throughout the day. In situations where you would maybe normally just react with a 'yes' or 'no' (without thinking), pause and ask yourself 'what do I really want to do right now?' Rediscovering your ability to make choices about your life – even the small bits – is empowering and will make answering the bigger questions so much easier. Do I want to go to the gym after work, or go for a drink? Do I want to meet friends later, or would I rather go home and relax? Just get used to asking yourself questions, and noticing what happens and how you feel in response.

SEARCHING FOR CLUES

Get a pen and paper (or your notebook) and brainstorm: write down all the things you enjoy, the things you love doing, your dreams and fantasies, your passions, hobbies, interests and wishes. You don't need to edit your writing or worry about it making sense – just fill your page or pages with things that make you feel good and then search these for clues about what you want more of in your life. Commit to writing for 15 minutes and keep your pen moving non-stop.

Here are some Thoughts and Questions to help you:

Think about the places and times you feel most at ease and in the flow.

What activities increase your energy levels?

Recall the times in your life when your health has been at its best – what was happening then? What were you doing?

What subject(s) fire you up?

What can you enthuse and talk endlessly about?   ▶

What are your favourite movies?

What kind of books do you lose yourself in?

What moves you?

Is there anything you do that makes you lose yourself and forget what time it is?

Are there people you admire and respect (you don't have to know them personally)?

Who inspires you? What qualities do they have that you so admire? Are these qualities that you want to have more of yourself?

Look at your answers for clues to things you would like more of in your life and directions you would like to explore.

A brand new Porsche

When asked what they really want a lot of people come up with variations on the following themes:

A brand new Porsche.

An exotic holiday.

One million pounds/euros/dollars.

A bigger house – with a swimming pool.

The perfect partner.

If your answer(s) match with any of the above, then a little more investigation is required to find out what you *really* want. I'm not for one minute disputing your desire for the above (or similar), but I am suggesting that there is something deeper that you really want, something that you believe having the above will give to you – and you can have it right now! Sound interesting? Then we need to ask a few more questions. Let's look at a couple of 'real' examples, and then you can apply the same line of questioning to help you discover what *you really* want:

JOHN'S ANSWER

In answer to the question 'What do you *really* want?', John said he wanted a brand new Porsche.

Q: If you had a *brand new Porsche*, what would that give you?
A: Something to impress people with.

Q: So, if you had something to impress people with, what would that give you?
A: I'd feel important.

Q: So, if you felt important, what would that give you?
A: I'd feel good about myself.

Q: So, if you felt good about yourself, what would that give you?
A: Confidence.

Q: So, if you felt confident, what would that give you?
A: I'd feel safe in the world.

Q: And if you felt safe in the world, what would that give you?
A: Peace.

KATHRYN'S ANSWER

Kathryn answered the same question and said she really wanted the perfect partner.

Q: If you had *the perfect partner*, what would that give you?
A: A hassle-free life.

Q: So, if you had a hassle-free life, what would that give you?
A: I'd feel safe and secure.

Q: So, if you felt safe and secure, what would that give you?
A: Happiness.

So for John, Porsche equals Peace and for Kathryn, the Perfect Partner equals Happiness. Whereas John might not have the money for a brand new Porsche at the moment, he can have peace right now – for free! And though Kathryn has not yet met her perfect partner, she can have Happiness today. Peace and happiness can be had **right now**. And can you see how if John or Kathryn felt that way now they might get the things they desire sooner? If John felt more peaceful he might find himself in a better position to earn the money for his car, and if Kathryn was happier she might attract the partner she desires. If you want to get something in order to feel a certain way, feeling that way now may be the fastest way for you to get whatever it is.

Peace and happiness can be had right now

CREATE PEACE OR HAPPINESS (OR WHATEVER ELSE YOU WISH TO FEEL) NOW

The first time you do any of the following exercises, find yourself somewhere comfortable and quiet where you can sit uninterrupted for a while. Relax your body, take a few deep calming breaths and close your eyes. This is YOUR time. With practice you will be able to recall the exercises and do them anywhere, but I would still recommend giving yourself some special quiet time for them whenever possible.

- Can you remember a time when you felt really peaceful/happy (or whatever else you wish to feel)? Recall that time now, fully experience it in your mind and body: see what you saw, feel what you felt, smell what you smelt, hear what you heard. Those feelings are yours – they do not belong to a particular time and place, you can have them whenever you want them. Recall them for a few moments, and practise recalling them until you can create the feeling at any time.

▶

- Do you know someone who is really peaceful/happy (or whatever else you wish to feel)? Imagine you are them. Can you imagine being really peaceful/happy? Act like someone who is really peaceful or happy. How do they look? How do they move? How do they speak? How do they feel? How do you feel if you 'be' that way?

- Meditate, laugh a lot, listen to music, do whatever it takes to create the feeling you desire.

- Can you imagine yourself being as peaceful/happy (or whatever else you wish to feel) as you desire? Create an image in your mind of that new you. How would you look? How would you feel? How would you move? What would you sound like? Make the picture as real and clear as possible. Wow! Look at you. Now step into the picture, step into the new you, just as if you were stepping into a new outfit.

Each time you do one of the above exercises make the image and the feeling bigger, brighter, clearer and stronger. Imagine you have a volume and brightness control, like on a TV, and adjust things till they are just how you want them to be. With practice you will be able to summon these feelings with ease – whenever you wish. And the more you do it the more the effect will linger and become part of your everyday life.

A PERFECT DAY

It's great to have all kinds of different goals, be they small and easily obtainable or huge and wild, but it's even greater to have an idea of what all of them together would mean for you. What life are you creating with these things that you really want? What would it be like to be living that life? A great way to do this is to imagine your ideal day. What would it be like? What would you be doing? Who would you ▶

be with? How would you feel? What would you look like? Take a pen and paper and create your ideal day. Find somewhere comfortable and peaceful to sit, a special place maybe where you feel safe, somewhere you can be uninterrupted for a while. Write everything down. From the moment you wake up on your perfect day, what would you see, feel, hear, smell. List everything that happens and add the detail. Be specific and dare to dream. Make this as real as possible and revisit this vision of your perfect day time and time again... until you are there!

Another great way to uncover what you really want is to ask yourself:

If you had three other lives to lead (or more if this feels limiting!) what would you do in them? What would you be? How would you be?

Would you be an explorer, a writer, a surgeon, a teacher, a gardener, a pop star?

Would you be adventurous, creative, technical, inspiring, confident?

Write down whatever pops into your mind – no censoring!

What elements of those other lives can you bring into your life right now?

 THINGS TO DO TODAY: Select one of your 'other lives' and write down some steps you can take towards exploring it this week. For instance, if you wrote down 'a sailor' you could organise a sailing lesson, buy a book about boats or take a walk near a harbour. If you wrote down 'peaceful' you could spend five minutes a day sitting in silence or walking in nature, buy a relaxation CD or join a local meditation group.

A visual reminder

Whether you've managed to answer the many questions posed in this chapter or not, whether your 'wants' list is pages long or still a 'work in progress', it can be helpful and inspiring to have a visual reminder of what you want. My favourite way to do this is to create a picture board – a visual feast of things that make me smile inside and out, an instant mood-lifter and changer. Friends and clients who have made their own versions report amazing results from their creations:

'If I ever feel despondent or down I just go look at my dream picture and take in every detail, within moments I feel better, back on track.'

'My picture is becoming less of a wish picture and more of an 'I have got picture' – it's amazing, life is beginning to look more and more like the picture.'

'I love my picture board, it inspires and motivates me daily.'

To make your own picture board get a piece of board or paper and cover it with pictures, quotes or even objects that make you smile – it's that simple. You can choose things that obviously depict and fit with your goals, or things that simply inspire you and appeal to you. I have had clients who have struggled with articulating their goals on lists, and have been unsure of what they really want – until they start cutting and pasting pictures! I suggest they arm themselves with a stack of colourful magazines/brochures and just leaf through and choose pictures they are drawn to. The results not only look good, they also provide information about what people really want.

'My picture board has been the singular most helpful thing for losing weight, getting healthy and fit. After years of trying numerous diets and getting nowhere I now just find myself eating healthy foods and taking more exercise. It is hard to believe that cutting pictures from magazines had such an effect, but I believe it was my catalyst for change.'

Life is happening right now, and your life is being created moment by moment by choices you are making. Results from all your actions are inevitable, and if you don't make the changes you want life will make them for you. It is often in the hard times that people change their direction in life and start doing something they've always felt an inner calling to do, or even something they'd never even thought of before. When things are rolling along ok they usually just talk about it and ponder possibilities, waiting, waiting, waiting for things to change. When the going gets tough people are often forced to overcome the doubts that hold them back. Divorce, the death of a loved one, redundancy, layoffs, illness, bankruptcy... times when you feel like there is nothing more to lose, or you just seem to have no choice – that's when people often muster incredible reserves and make life-changing decisions. Why wait? If you've an inner calling LISTEN TO IT! If you would like to do something different but have no idea what, then start to explore ideas NOW.

4

TODAY IS THE DAY ALL YOUR RELATIONSHIPS START TO IMPROVE

U nless you choose to go and live as a hermit, you are going to have relationships – with a partner, family, friends, boss, colleagues, neighbours… In fact, even if you did choose a life of solitude you would still have a relationship: with yourself. In this chapter we are going to look at what you can do to improve your relationships – including the one you have with yourself. The quality of your relationships often determines the quality of your life – at home, work and alone with yourself.

Would you like to feel self-confident and self-aware enough to be able to fully engage and connect with those around you; to get the best from your relationships – at home and work? This is one area of life where we can expend (and waste) enormous amounts of energy on worry, anxiety, confusion, fear, anger, bitterness, resentment and frustration… need I go on? And often the source of the most pain is our own wild imaginings. You can change that.

And when we are not imagining what we think others are thinking or feeling, we are busy taking personally whatever they may say. However, another's point of view springs entirely from their own upbringing, conditioning and life experiences – it is not about YOU. Take note next time someone makes a comment about you. If the comment is negative, it is most likely they themselves who are feeling unhappy, sad, mad or down on their luck. If it is a positive comment they are probably feeling happy, confident, at peace and up! People's comments are truly only reflections of how they are feeling. You can choose how to react.

Changing how we relate to others can be one of the most potent life-changers of all – and it can start today!

In this chapter a lot is written about 'love' relationships – since these tend to be the focal point for so many people. Whether you are single or perfectly happy with 'the love of your life' please read on, as the principles are universal. Whether you are looking to improve your relationships at work or with your family, simply alter the exercises to suit your needs.

Relationship ratings

A friend of mine recently confided that she had married the wrong man. Not by accident of course! And not recently either, they have been together for 15 years. She told me how the day he proposed a small voice inside her said 'no' several seconds before she heard the word 'yes' come out of her mouth. Why the heck did she do it then? Because she 'thought she loved him' and didn't want to be left on the shelf – they had been together for four years already and she couldn't imagine life without him, even though life with him was mediocre, to say the least. And why is she still with him? Because they have been together so long and she can't imagine life without him; even though life with him is now less than mediocre.

Two other friends of mine have been married for sixty years and there is no mistaking the twinkle in their eyes when they relate the story of their first meeting all those years ago. 'We've had our ups and downs', they'll say, 'but we've always talked things through and we respect one another.' 'And I still fancy her, that helps', he'll say with a cheeky grin; 'Oh give over you daft old fool', she'll reply (grinning and blushing like the teenager he fell in love with!).

I asked the above couples to rate their relationship on a scale of 1 to 10, where 1 equals 'a disaster' and 10 equals 'a match made in heaven'. (I only asked my one friend in the first relationship... asking both could have stirred up a hornet's nest that I hadn't been invited to stir!) Half of couple number one rated her relationship a 2, and couple number two both proclaimed theirs to be a 10 out of 10 marriage. How would you rate yours? Go on be honest... there is no point in being otherwise with yourself if you truly want to start making the most out of life.

So, NO analysing, judging, or questioning. Go with your first truthful response: on a scale of 1 to 10 where do you rate your relationship? (You can apply the same question to any other relationships – siblings, parents, your boss, your friends. Think about anybody you like and rate your relationship with them on a scale of 1 to 10.) Now, do you want to spend the rest of your life in a relationship with that score? If not, read on...

 THINGS TO DO TODAY: What would it take to move your relationship score up 1 on the scale? How would you need to be different? What could you do TODAY to make a change? And then how could you move it up 1 more...? And 1 more...?

If you scored low it doesn't necessarily mean you have to jump ship right away. But life is too short to be in a low-scoring relationship, so if change for the better is what you want, it does mean *doing something about it*. And you have three options for improvement:

1 Accept the relationship for what it is and get on with making the most of life (this means stopping wasting time and energy on resentment, regrets, bitterness, anger, self-pity... need I go on?).

2 Do something to improve the relationship.

3 Leave the relationship[1].

You, you, you

Whatever you do, remember this is about YOU – not the other person. '*What!?*', I hear you exclaim, '*Of course it's about him/ her... if he/she would only... it's his/her fault we are in this mess... if he/she would just change...*' I know it can be a hard truth to grasp,

---

[1] Please ignore this option if you happen to be thinking about a relationship with a parent, child or sibling. But please do read on...

but there is only one person you can change and that is you; and what a relief – because trying to change someone else is a fruitless and exhaustive process. If the above statement of blame rang true with you, then you've probably already exhausted yourself trying to change your partner and become more and more exasperated in the process. However, there is a kind of magic that takes place when you start to change you – the people around you suddenly become different too.

It's not rocket science. How do you feel when you are with someone who is happy in themselves? And how do you feel when you are with someone who is always unhappy with their lot? Of course it affects you – and likewise how *you* are affects others, bringing out the best or worst in them. How you are affects you, too… you spend more time with yourself than with anyone else, so how would *you* like yourself to be? Freedom comes from knowing that we can only change our lives from the inside out, and the same is true of our relationships.

You spend more time with yourself than with anyone, so how would *you* like yourself to be?

WHAT'S MISSING?

My guess is that if you are unhappy in your relationship then you probably feel like 'the other' is not giving you something you need, there is something missing. Write five things you want but are not getting from your partner (and yes you can do this exercise for any relationship: family, friends, colleagues… though please note the examples below are not great ones for the workplace!).

For example:

1 I want to be touched more
2 I want romance

▶

3 I want to be listened to

4 I want to feel loved

5 I want breakfast in bed on a Sunday

Now here are two radical ideas:

RADICAL IDEA NUMBER 1:

Give to your partner what it is you want and see what happens! Read through your list and ask yourself – are you doing YOUR best on all five counts within your relationship? Honestly? There is a saying, 'We get back what we give'. So... If you want to be touched more, do more touching: give your partner a shoulder massage, hold hands and put your arm around them. If it's romance you're after, be romantic: make dinner a special occasion, light some candles and take a moonlit walk. If you want to be heard, ask your partner how they are feeling/how their day was/what their wildest dreams are – and do some listening. If you want to feel loved, be more loving. If it's breakfast in bed you're after, surprise your partner with just that.

RADICAL IDEA NUMBER 2:

Give to yourself what you feel is missing. If you want to be touched more, book yourself a massage, shiatsu, reflexology session. If it's romance you want then buy a good book or rent a good movie... indulge yourself! If you want to be listened to, call a good trusted friend and arrange a night out – or in – and talk, talk, talk... or call a counsellor. Feeling loved is really an inside job anyway, so ask yourself: what would help you to feel loved? What does being loved really mean for you? Give yourself love! Yes, you can do it. (Breakfast in bed? OK, so you may have to leave the warmth of the covers for a while, but you can do that for yourself.)

I asked a random sample of people what qualities (other than looks!) drew them to people. The top answer by far was 'someone who is a good listener', second was 'sense of humour' and third was 'a positive attitude'. What qualities draw you to someone? And how can you bring more of these qualities to the fore in your own life (remember: like attracts like)? Listening is a crucial part of communication; often people think they are communicating when they are really only talking and making assumptions. True

Listening improves all relationships

listening requires you to set aside distractions from your mind, to be fully present rather than thinking about what you have to do later, what happened earlier or what you 'imagine' to be happening now. Listening is a sign of affirmation and improves all relationships – so there is little wonder it scored so high in my mini-poll.

 THINGS TO DO TODAY: Really listen when someone speaks to you – be it your partner/child/colleague/friend/a stranger. You will both gain. They will feel affirmed and heard; you will have enhanced your relationship with them. And you might actually learn something about them too.

Know what you want

Before making any change in any relationship we need to know what it is we *do* want. If you've no idea where you're headed you'll just keep going round in circles, corkscrewing yourself deeper into a hole, and your scores are more likely to go down than up. It is oh so easy to go on and on about what we don't want – and how miserable does that make us feel? Focusing on all that is wrong in your relationship is not going to help you feel any better. Acknowledging that life isn't as rosy as you would like it to be is a great first step, but if you want to move forwards then focusing ahead is the best way.

Do you know what you want?

Do you have a vision for your 10 out of 10 relationship?

What would it be like?

RELATIONSHIP VISION

Imagine you wake up one morning and your relationship is perfect (you can apply this to any relationship). How would you know it is perfect? What would be happening? How would it feel? What would you see? What would you hear? Get a pen and paper and start writing a list of sentences that describe your 'perfect relationship'. Go on, let your imagination run wild, be as specific as you can. This is your foundation for change, your base from which to build upon. Start every sentence with I or we (not he or she), phrase everything positively (i.e. what you do want, not what you don't want) and write it in the present tense, as if it is already happening (for example 'we have fun together').

If you're unsure where to begin, start by writing about a perfect day in your relationship, and then expand it to your vision for a week, a month, a lifetime...

For example (for a romantic relationship):

I always wake up feeling peaceful and relaxed.

We wake up and have great sex.

We spend some time talking before getting on with the day (and all this before breakfast!).

You may find it easy to write your list, or it may take some time. If you are not accustomed to stating what you want in love and imagining the very best, you may find yourself a little rusty at first. It's a bit like flexing a muscle that hasn't been used for a while... keep going and it will get easier.

Relationships are as different and varied as the people in them. Just as there are no two people exactly alike, there are no two relationships exactly alike and what works for one may well not work for another. Shared vision and values are probably two of the most important elements in a 'successful' love relationship. If you dream of being self-sufficient on a small-holding, surrounded by loads of kids and animals, and your partner dreams of a neat and tidy townhouse with regular champagne dinners, then it probably ain't gonna work.

WHAT WOULD YOU SAY?

Find yourself a quiet spot/moment and imagine yourself ten years from now. Imagine that life is fantastic and you are in an amazing relationship (it may be with the same partner you are with now), you feel fulfilled and happy and all that has gone before is history. What would the wiser, older you say to the you of today? What advice would the 'future you' offer?

Wishing that a partner would change to better suit your needs will only lead to frustration. Your own self-esteem is the primary source of real confidence and security. If you do not feel emotionally whole, it is tempting to expect someone else to fill the void. But the best relationships are not a guard against loneliness – they are there to enjoy for what positive things they can bring to the mix. If fear of loneliness or insecurity is affecting your relationship, look for ways you can change and help yourself. Maybe that could go on your goal list in Chapter 6 – along with doable clear steps to achieve the self-esteem you desire, and deserve.

 THINGS TO DO TODAY: if you were to write down one goal to change or improve a relationship that is important to you, what would it be? My goal is to ·

What first step could you take today?
And if you were to write down one goal for your own personal growth – your relationship with yourself – what would it be? ▶

My goal is to

_____

What first step could you take today?

_____

Acceptance

Acceptance is one of the greatest gifts you can give to anyone –
acceptance of how they are and who they are. How different would
your relationship be with your partner, your parents, siblings,
in-laws, children, friends, colleagues, if you just accepted them as
they are – with no desire to change or advise, criticise or judge?

MISUNDERSTANDINGS

He (with memories of being ignored in the past when he was in
trouble, believes he is responsible for how others feel):
'She ignored me, I have obviously done or said something wrong, oh
my, this is not going to make for an easy day. Actually I feel quite
mad about that – she could have the decency to tell me what is
wrong rather than give me a hard time. Well two can play at that
game. I'll act like I didn't notice, like I am not bothered.'

She (with memories of being in trouble for forgetting to do
things, believes she may be punished for her carelessness):
'I was at the shops, then the garage, where else did I go? Damn,
I can't believe I dropped those gloves somewhere, they were my
favourites. Should I go back? Where was I last wearing them? Oh this is
driving me mad, I need to forget about it till later. Maybe I should check
my bag again. Oh, I didn't see him come in! Oh dear, he looks mad, what
have I done wrong? Better not tell him about the gloves right now.'

We can never fully understand what goes on in another's mind and we can never have access to their memories and resultant beliefs. Everyone lives in their own world – even those we love and know well. Imagining we always know what they are thinking or feeling is a futile exercise and can lead to the overuse of our own imagination based upon our own memories and beliefs.

THINGS TO DO TODAY: Become aware of times when you negatively 'imagine' what another is thinking or feeling (at home or work). Notice how your imagining makes you feel and behave. How does that enhance or detract from the relationship? Always make your first assumption that their 'perceived mood' has nothing to do with you. If the roles were reversed, how would you like to be greeted or treated? Remain positive or neutral and use your imagination for something more positive.

Mirrors

The starting point towards more deeply satisfying relationships with others is your relationship with yourself, and you can improve this by developing an understanding of how you respond to people and situations, why you think and behave as you do, and where you first got the ideas and beliefs that you live your life by (often as way back as childhood).

One way to find out more is to take notice of how people are around you, based on the premise that they just may be reflecting your own innermost beliefs (beliefs you may not even be aware you have) by treating you how you feel about yourself. Look around you as if life was holding up a mirror – what can you learn by what you see coming back at you?

If you are feeling positive and you are supporting people, then it's likely that you will find yourself among positive and supportive people. What kind of people are you attracting in your life today? Are there common themes in your relationships?

For instance, if you find that your relationships always fail in a specific way (they always say that you don't love them enough), everyone is always late for meetings with you, or that people seem to keep putting you down, you may need to do a little soul searching and ask yourself, 'Deep down, how do I feel about myself?'

 THINGS TO DO TODAY: Identify a pattern in your life – what keeps happening that results in you feeling not OK? What is the most common criticism/judgement that comes your way? What persistently annoys, hurts or frustrates you about the way others are around you?

Examples	Questions you might ask yourself
People frequently let me down.	How do you let yourself or others down?
Partners always cheat on me.	How are you not valuing yourself?
People get angry with me.	What are you angry about?
Colleagues seem secretive.	Am I holding things back from them?

Treat yourself as you would like others to treat you – and be aware of the messages and signals you are giving to others. A small change can make a huge difference in turning around such patterns. Sometimes awareness itself can be curative.

Don't make assumptions. If you do not understand – ask questions.

MIRROR, MIRROR IN MY LIFE

Think of someone who really 'pushes your buttons', someone you are having problems relating to, someone who is driving you a little nuts at the moment. Take a piece of paper and divide it into two vertical columns. At the top of the left column write: Things I *do not* like about xxx. At the top of the right column write: Things I *do* like about xxx. Now get writing. Be honest (you are not going to show this to anyone!), and as much as you may struggle with the right-hand column if you are feeling strong negative feelings towards this person at the moment, do see if you can identify at least a few positive qualities.

Example:

Things I *do not* like about xxx	Things I *do* like about xxx
Selfish	Focused
Self-centred	Disciplined
Uncaring	Independent
Negative	
Arrogant	

When you've completed your list, I want you to cross out the other person's name at the top and replace it with your own. How do you react when you do that? Can you see any truth in there? Is it possible that you do display those negative characteristics – even in a much smaller way? And the positive qualities – are they ones you can own or would like to develop? There is a saying: that we can only recognise in others what we see in ourselves. Other people can be our teachers, teaching us things about ourselves – and sometimes the ones we have the most to learn from are the ones who 'push our buttons' the most.

THINGS TO DO TODAY: What relationships would you like to attract into your life? List some key qualities or types of relationships you would like to bring into your life. Take one of those qualities and bring it to the fore in your interactions with others today. Adopt the quality for yourself and BE the change!

In Chapter 6 you are going to start setting your goals and taking action to reach them. What goals have you identified while reading through this chapter? How would you like to change your relationships? Here are a few examples from other people's goal lists; sometimes other people's goals can spark our own ideas and get us started:

> To make my peace with ...
> Develop better communication with my children.
> To go on a date with my wife at least once a month.
> To become a better listener.
> To spend more time with myself.
> To stop arguing.
> To find my soul mate.
> To find new friends who are uplifting to be with.

5

TODAY IS THE DAY YOU MAKE YOUR WORKING LIFE WORK FOR YOU

Some part of you knows how you really want work to be, or what work you really want to do – but are you listening? This chapter is going to encourage you to listen to yourself: to dig deep and find your own buried reserves, riches and resources; to bring to light your talents, gifts, abilities and dreams. You may want to change how you are at work, to change how work is for you, or to stop what you're doing and go for a complete change. Whatever change you desire, you can start it today.

MISSED OPPORTUNITIES

I once heard a story about a man who was retiring from a lifetime's employment as an insurance salesman. He had started out as a trainee fresh from school with the intention of working a few years, just long enough to make enough money to set up his own business. That had been almost 50 years ago! The company organised a leaving-do and his boss presented him with a gift. The man unwrapped his gift and broke down in tears. It was a beautiful gold clock. The business he had dreamed of starting-up was a clock shop; for as long as he could remember he had wanted to make clocks.

Then there's the woman who worked as a supervisor in a factory making frozen meals. As with many jobs, hers had become more and more pressured as the years went by and she found herself managing more staff, on a tighter budget, with evermore demanding deadlines. For weeks she had been feeling breathless and unwell, but did not dare take time off. Then one day she collapsed halfway through her shift. She had had a heart attack. During her time in hospital she confided in one of the nurses that ever since being a little girl she too had wanted to be a nurse, but her teachers had dissuaded her!

Let's make sure your hopes and dreams don't get left by the wayside or squashed by other people.

As a parent I have only one wish for my child in his future and that is that he be happy and healthy doing whatever he chooses, whatever that may be. I know a lot of parents feel exactly the same way. I wonder, did our parents have the same wishes for us when we were carefree toddlers? So *what* happens? I wonder if the parents of the clock man and never nurse wanted them to be happy doing something they loved? And I wonder if *their* children wound up doing things they loved? As parents the best way to lead is by example: to follow our passions; to do things we love doing; to wake up every morning excited by the day ahead. Actually that's how many of us started out as children.

Of course many people are only too quick to blame their parents for their own unhappy work situation.

'They wanted me to follow in the family business.'

'All I ever understood is that work was supposed to be hard.'

'They nagged me about choosing the "right" job.'

'I was dissuaded from doing what I wanted because it wasn't "sensible".'

'They laughed at my dream of being a musician.'

The affects of parental pressure on vulnerable children and teenagers is unquestionable. If we have no other role models then

Your life is now

it's tough to break the mould and do something different, to stand alone and make a stand. BUT, that is in the past, it is done, gone. Your life is now and when you drop your story and allow yourself to be who you are right now, you instantly become more alive and inspired. You are not your parents. You are not your story. You do not have to replicate their beliefs about work. This is your life, right now, right here. Your choices so far (be they made under pressure or not) have led you to where you are. If you want to change direction, steer another course or choose another destination, you can do so by making different choices.

In the right job?

Life is too short to be in the wrong job. Five or six days a week, 40-plus weeks a year, for most of your adult life... as one corporate executive I worked with commented: 'It's like a life sentence'. But work need not be drudgery, it can be exciting, fun, inspiring, it can be play, service, love – it can be something you really WANT to do three, four, five or six days a week, 40-plus weeks a year for the rest of your life.

Are you 'sick of your work'? Listen to the call before it shouts too loud. Many people do not pay attention to their own unhappiness, frustration or even illness as a call to make a change. Stoically they carry on as normal as though such things are an expected part of a busy, 'full' life. Tracey was away ill from her work on-and-off for three months; each time her health improved a bit she returned, but each time she fell ill again within a short space of time. It was only her doctor's seemingly glib comment one day that she was maybe 'sick of work' that turned a light on for her. I have coached people who have stated that their 'illnesses have changed their lives' – I would rather you didn't have to go that far.

YES OR NO

Answer the following five questions with a yes or no as quickly as possible. I want your first answers, the truthful answers that spring from within... not ones you feel you ought to give, or ones you have had time to think through. Be honest, there is little point in being otherwise with yourself if you truly want to change your work life: ▶

1 Do you love your work?

2 Do you wake up full of energy for the day ahead?

3 Does your job give you more than money/car/benefits?

4 Would you keep doing what you are doing now if you won millions on the lottery?

5 If you could live your life again would you follow the same career path?

Was it 'yes' to all five questions? Would you like it to be? If there were any 'no' answers were they accompanied by a feeling? What was the feeling? Some examples people have cited are: resignation, anger, bitterness, sadness. Is that feeling (or feelings) with you everyday you go to work? Or have you managed to suppress it (in which case it is still there in some form – sorry).

Is it time for a change? Ask yourself:
'If I could apply for any job, enjoy any career, or start any business *and be guaranteed success*, what would it be?'

 THINGS TO DO TODAY: send your future self an email. Imagine you are mailing yourself in the future (10, 20, 30 years from now) – what questions would you ask your future self?

Examples: Did you go for that job you really wanted?

Did you make a career change?

Did you find the work you love to do?

Did you re-study?

Did you work on your confidence/assertiveness/leadership/delegating?

▶

You don't have to answer these questions; the very act of thinking of the questions you would like to ask can have a powerful effect on you and encourage you to reassess your life today. Take note of the questions you ask and which ones carry the greatest emotional charge.

Or imagine you are a child again and emailing (writing to) yourself in the future (10, 20, 30 years onwards). Remind the you of today about what you wanted to be when you were a child, what you loved doing and what you dreamed about for the future. Did you want to be a musician? An explorer? A scientist? A teacher? Did you love painting? Making things? Being outdoors? Writing stories? Having adventures? Revive those childhood dreams – they may provide valuable pointers to what you 'really' want to be doing now.

SITUATIONS VACANT

List five (or more) negative words that best describe your work and your feelings about your work. Here are some examples from others who have done this exercise that may help to get you going:

boring

frustrating

horrid

tedious

waste of time

pressured

scary

►

Now rearrange the words you have listed to write an advertisement for your job. For example:

Company seeking boring person to do frustrating work in a horrid environment. Tedious job that feels like a waste of time, with lots of pressure and a very scary boss. Interested? Please call...

Would you apply?

Now write five or more positive words that you would least associate with your work and your experience of work. Or, put another way: five or more positive words you would love to associate with your work. Here are some examples to help inspire you:

fulfilling

exciting

fun

stimulating

inspiring

lovely

Now rearrange the words you have listed to write an advertisement for a job. For example:

Company seeks an exciting and fun person to join them in this lovely, inspiring business. Fulfilling and stimulating work awaits the right person. Interested? Please call...

Does this sound like a job for you?

Hopefully both adverts made you smile – for very different reasons! My guess is the words you chose for job number two are significant to you, so keep them to hand, write them down and post them

▶

somewhere you can see them regularly. Let them awaken you to new possibilities and inspire you to make changes.

'But I've got to pay the bills!'

Yes, I know. But what if you could be one of the lucky ones who gets to do something you love and still manages to pay the bills? People do it. Some make radical career changes and earn lots more money. Some make radical changes and earn less but are SO much happier that it isn't an issue.

I asked ten random people why they do the work they do. Nine of them did it mainly for the money – 'to pay the bills'. The odd one out did it because she loves it, and even though she earns less than the other nine she is the happiest! I asked the nine to think of a word to describe how they felt about working just to pay the bills. Five said 'resentful', two said 'angry', two said 'resigned'. I then asked them all to say whether they felt their feelings about their work had a positive or negative impact on their relationships with their families. Six said they felt their experiences at work had a negative impact on how they were at home, three said it varied depending on the type of day they had.

Do you want to spend the rest of your life doing something you don't love doing? If yes, skip to the next chapter, if no, read on.

Magical things occur when we make an internal shift

If changing your job seems like too big a mountain to climb right now, then how about changing your attitude to your work? You can do that right NOW! And magical things occur when we make an internal shift – the universe listens and responds in amazing ways.

Smile!! Smile at your colleagues, customers, and the people you meet on the way to and from work. Research with depressed people has shown that the very act of smiling (even if you don't feel happy inside) has a profound effect on how you feel. All those smile muscles send 'happy' signals to your brain and before long you feel smiley inside, too. And people prefer to be around someone who smiles a lot, so colleagues and customers will be different with you. Go on, force yourself if you have to.

Do whatever you do to the very best of your ability. Give it your 100 per cent attention. Take pride in your work. Focus on the detail and be the best '(*enter your job title here*)' ever. You'll be amazed how this affects those around you, too.

Be fully present. If you spend your days mulling over what happened this morning or how you're going to get done what you need to get done this evening, then you're going to tire yourself out and time will seem to drag. A state of 'flow' (when time just passes by and you don't even notice) can only be achieved by being fully present – in the moment. It also prevents you from making mental mountains out of mental molehills!

Be yourself! Pretending to be someone you're not is exhausting and soul-destroying. What percentage of your 'self' do you take to work? Being true to yourself moment to moment, wherever you are, whatever you are doing, is one of the greatest gifts you can give to yourself. It also inspires other people to do the same – what a gift! Authenticity is inspiring.

Authenticity is inspiring

Make change happen

If you want something to change then you have to make a change. You may feel trapped by your work because of your financial situation, but it is truly only your thinking that has you trapped. If change for the better is what you want, it does mean *doing something about it*. And you have three options for improvement.

1. Accept

Accept your work for what it is and get on with making the most of life (this means stopping wasting time and energy on resentment, bitterness, anger, self-pity… need I go on?). Compare how much time you spend thinking about what you don't like about your existing work situation with how much time you spend exploring how you could make it better – imagining new possibilities! Tip the balance in your favour and put your attention where it will best help you. Look for opportunities instead of problems. Be creative rather than bored. And what about looking to other areas of your life to re-ignite your interests – a new hobby, club, group, interest, activity? How you feel about one area of your life permeates all other areas of your life, so having more fun outside of work could help you at work, too.

2. Do something to improve your work situation

Have you become stuck in a negative spiral, focusing on all that is 'wrong' with your current work situation and ignoring all that is 'right'? How can you turn that around? Notice ten things to be grateful for in your work right now – today. Write a list of ten talents, qualities and skills you have. Do you utilise those assets in your existing position? Could you? What would have to change for that to happen? How could you put one of those skills to work today? What else could you do? Re-design your workspace? Talk to your boss? Spend more time with people who do enjoy their work, people who are inspiring and positive? Stop comparing yourself to others in the workplace – you have your own set of skills and qualities that you take to work – be yourself, to the best of your ability.

If moving on is not an option for you right now, what can you do instead? Can you change how you feel about what you are doing? Think outside the box. Imagine something whacky – how about standing on Uranus with a giant telescope and looking at your work situation from there? Your brain has no concept of such a possibility, so it has to work out new ways of thinking to imagine it – new neural pathways. We are all born with the ability to use our whole brain, but school and work often encourage us to become more left-brained, using logic to problem-solve. Thinking innovatively and creatively will change how you feel – a major first step to creating the change you desire.

3. Leave the job

Many people spend lifetimes working at jobs they do not like, while spending any spare hours (or even those un-spare work ones) figuring out what they would rather do instead. Lists are made, books are read, grand schemes are hatched, dreams are dreamt, but nothing changes. If you have done your best to make the most of what you have, if you have given it your best shot and been the best you can be, yet still you are unhappy and unfulfilled at work, then maybe it is time to move on. Yes, write lists, read books, hatch schemes and dream – but don't make a career of it! Use this book as an action plan rather than as a set of ideas. Decide what you don't want, what you do want, set active goals, take steps, master you own mind and make changes – starting now.

Work and career goals often feature highly on goal lists. Start thinking now about what your goals are, because soon you will be taking your first steps to achieving them. They can be as grandiose or not as you wish – they are *your* goals and will only remain as words on paper if they are not what you really want.

SETTING THE RIGHT GOALS

Steve had been on several goal-setting-type seminars and workshops during his ten years in his job, but little had changed. 'I always felt like I had to have massive dreams and ideals when I was on the workshops – about earning mega money, major promotions or doing something out of the ordinary. So I made some goals that felt a little exciting at the time, but I guess I never really wanted any of them. It was only one day out with some mates that I realised that actually I just wanted to better enjoy what I was doing. When I made that a goal it was easy.'

Susan had always wanted to work in medicine but had lacked self-confidence and opted for a civil service job that she had grown to hate. 'We used to talk about goals at work, but they were always focused on what we were already doing and the promotions we might get to do more of the same – rather than anything radical. Then one night I read a magazine article about some youngster who was off to study psychiatry and there was an 'older' student in her group too. I had thought it was way too late in my life to switch career, but there and then I knew I had to do it – or regret it forever. My goal was clear and now here I am – loving my work and, with my maturity, more able to cope with some things than my younger colleagues.'

Here are some sample work/career goals to help get you thinking:

To find a different career.

To reach a sales goal of...

To stop taking work home in the evening/at the weekend.

To attend evening classes.

To find a way to only work three days a week.

To find new clients each month.

To write a plan for my daily activities.

To seek the help of a business coach.

To always get my reports done on time.

To find a business I can run from home.

To get promoted.

To improve my self-confidence in meetings.

6

TODAY IS THE DAY YOU SET GOALS AND MAKE PLANS

In this chapter you'll learn how to take all your 'do not wants' (Chapter 2), 'things to change' and 'do wants' (Chapter 3), your 'relationship dreams' (Chapter 4) and 'work ideas' (Chapter 5) and turn them into an action-packed Goal List (rather than an inactive one that requires nothing more than writing and hoping things will turn out OK). In order to make the changes and create the future you want, you have to set goals – without them the future will choose for you. It's time to start a little life-alchemy; to transform what you already have into something so much better. If you are still not clear about what your goals are, you are in good company – for many it is the very act of writing down what they truly want that finally unleashes a wellspring of ideas and possibilities from within. Let the alchemy begin.

The last five chapters will have got you thinking and dreaming – and if you have started implementing small daily changes you will already be noticing a shift occurring. It's time now to draw together all the things you have identified as areas to change, to ask yourself what you would do with your life if you could wave a magic wand and do anything you choose – with guaranteed success. You may have spent many years dreaming of change and formulating ideas, but today you are going to put them into action. It is worth noting the date – because the writing of your Goal List may well be a day to remember – the day your life changed for the better.

What makes a good goal list?

Most people spend more time making a list for the supermarket than they do making a list of the things they really want in life. Studies have shown that fewer than six per cent of us bother to write down our life goals. And of those that do write them down, only a small percentage actually achieve their goals. I know a few people who write down the same goals year after year (often on their birthdays or the beginning of a new year). They never accomplish their goals, so they write them down again the next year. But what makes a good goal list? What makes one that works?

Successful goal-setters (people who routinely set and achieve goals) agree that goals need to be clear, specific, positive and measurable. They must be things that you really desire and believe you can have. They must also include action steps: things to do today, next week and next month to move you towards your goal. These action steps are probably the most important part of your goal list – without them you will have no plan, no map, no idea how to get there. And it is these small steps that make *today* the day you change your life!

Goals need to be clear, specific, positive and measurable

A mere list of words on paper is not going to get you what you want either – you have to 'do something'. And you have to believe in the words you write and be able to imagine them coming to life. This is why it is so important that your list of words be truly yours; imbued with feeling and meaning, they must focus you and/or fire you with excitement and passion. Your feelings and imagination and energy are the fuel you need to get to where you want to be. And your goal list is your atlas, a way to get you to where you want to be. Read and act upon them regularly and you'll be programming your own personal sat-nav to success.

Different choices = different outcomes

You can only make the best choices if you know where you're headed, otherwise it's a little like shooting in the dark and hoping for the best. Without specific goals to follow your mind will keep following programmes from the past and listening to the myriad random messages it receives daily. When a goal is identified and you know what to do next, then you are able to make life-changing choices.

JUST A COINCIDENCE?

Goal lists also act like tracking devices. Write something down and often synchronicity comes into play. A friend of mine, Kim, had always been interested in animals, but she worked 'uninterestedly' with computers and their hard drives. Unsure of the validity of writing a goal list, she decided to give it a go one evening. But nothing came out of the pen. What did she want? Just then her two dogs got into a fight (nothing too major) and she heard herself asking, 'What did you do that for?' With peace resumed she picked up her blank piece of paper once again and found herself writing: 'I want to learn more about animal behaviour'.

Despite the fact that she had been struggling about what to write on her list, she felt strangely excited about the prospect of her newly penned goal. 'I got butterflies in my stomach and felt more positive than I had for ages.' The very next day Kim's car refused to start, so she made a dash for the bus instead – where she sat on a seat containing a leaflet about an animal behaviour course at a local college!

This kind of experience is partly a function of selective attention. Have you ever learned a word you've never heard before, and then heard it numerous times over the next week? Or seen an advert for a car you'd really like, and then seen several said cars on the road? If your mind is focused on a particular thing it will sort through the infinite amounts of information you receive every day and hone in on things relating to your subject of interest. Writing down what you want and making it real by fuelling it with energy and imagination preps your brain to find related things in the world around you. And maybe partly it is magic. Whatever it is – it works!

Past goals

If you have set goals in the past and either not achieved them, or stalled halfway (or less), you may be wincing a bit at the idea of trying again. Well you are not going to 'try' again – this time you are going to do it in a pro-active way. Trying is not doing. Have a go at this: try to smile. Did you try? Now actually SMILE. The difference between trying and doing is like the difference between black and white – the two do not compare. Trying does not get you what you want. Doing does!

If you have a goal that you've been trying to achieve for some years with no success, you need to ask yourself do you *really* want it? Is it really your goal or something you feel you 'should' do? If there are any shoulds, ought-tos, must-dos, have-tos involved in making your list then I suggest you think again (and scrap them). Replace them with wants, desires, aims, aspire-tos, would-likes, intentions and gonna-gets!

If the answer is 'Yes I really do want it' then let's explore what has stopped you. Look at the example below and insert your own answers in place of the suggestions.

MY GOAL IS
To find a different career from the one I am now in.

WHAT DO YOU WANT THIS GOAL FOR? (WHAT WILL IT GIVE YOU?)
Job satisfaction. More money. Sense of purpose. Better work/life balance.

WHAT HAS STOPPED YOU FROM ACHIEVING IT SO FAR?
Been too busy at work. Have not explored options. Don't know where to start.

WHAT HAS STOPPED YOU DOING THINGS TO HELP
YOU ACHIEVE IT?
Unsure of myself - lack of confidence. Afraid to
fail. Not sure what else I am capable of doing.

WHAT DO YOU NEED TO FOCUS ON TO ACHIEVE THIS
GOAL?
Improving my confidence. Listing my strengths and
abilities. Finding some small steps to take that
are less scary than one major change. Researching
other career options to see what appeals.

ARE YOU COMMITTED TO DOING THIS?
Yes.
Bingo!

Your mind is a powerful tool and a goal list gives it a job to do. With something clear to aim at, it can focus and direct you to reach an intended goal. With nothing to aim for its energy is misspent and wasted. Clearly defined goals direct your thinking and your actions.

If a goal is not written down it is a wish, a hope or a want – not a real goal. Research has shown that the chance of attaining a goal that is not committed to paper is as low as five per cent. However, when a goal is written down, clearly imagined, believable and broken down into action steps, the chances increase to as much as 75 per cent.

THINGS TO DO TODAY: Write down a very short-term goal: something you want to do tomorrow, or the next day. Write it down and include the date you want to achieve this goal by. Now write down the steps you need to take in order to realise your goal.

For instance:
My goal is to arrange a night out with friends on Saturday.

Steps to reach goal:

1 Check my diary to make sure I have nothing else arranged for Saturday – or early Sunday!

2 Decide where to go and at what time.

3 Decide who to invite.

4 Invite friends.

That is how easy goal-setting is. If you trip up on any of the steps (diary double-booked, friends not available) then redefine your goal (go out next Saturday, invite someone different).

How to write a pro-active goal list

1. Know what you want. Remember goals are not just about career and money. You may find it useful to start with headlines for areas of your life: health and fitness, family, relationships, home-life, travel/adventure, personal growth, friends, education, contribution to society, social-life/pleasure, fun, spirituality, career, finances/money, 'others'.

2. Start each goal with the word 'to'. This way you are making a very clear and committed statement:
(My goal is) to...

3. Be as specific and clear as possible. The more real your description, the more you will prep your brain to find what you need and create your dream. For instance: '(My goal is) to be debt-free and have £250,000 in the bank' will work better than '(My goal is) to have more money'.

4. Wherever possible state your goal in positive terms. Say what it is you DO want – rather than what you don't want. For instance: '(My goal is) to weigh 150 pounds', not '(My goal is) to stop weighing 200 pounds'.

5. Make sure you really want this goal. Now that may sound obvious, but be sure this goal is for YOU, not to please anyone else or to look good or prove a point. If you are having trouble writing the goal down, feeling like you are having to force yourself to do it, then it may be time to re-examine that goal.

6. All your goals must have an intended target date. Estimate when you expect to reach your goals: six months, one year, two years, five, ten, twenty years. Vague 'whenevers' are not going to focus you and help you achieve your goals.

7. Goals must be flexible (and that means their target dates, too). 'Gasp!' That probably sounds like it goes against everything that has ever been said about goals (how can you commit to something if it might change?), but one of the prime reasons people do not achieve their goals is because they don't update them or alter them as necessary. Life changes, ideas change, influences change – be prepared to be flexible and review your goals regularly. This doesn't mean giving yourself get-out clauses when the going gets tricky – it means honestly appraising when something is no longer viable and needs adjusting.

So we have looked at goals and how to set them, at the feelings required for fuelling any action and at the 'magic' of setting your brain radar. But you want change now, right? The very action of identifying and setting goals is a change in itself for many – but let's be more specific and start taking baby steps right now.

The action steps are what get us to our goals. Yes, passion, desire, dreams, excitement, enthusiasm, zest and downright craziness can help to move mountains – but nothing quite beats well-planned and well-executed steps taken at regular intervals. They don't burn you out, or over-stretch you, they are not scary or too daunting, but they are progress and movement, and as such they inspire and motivate you and make you feel good about yourself.

THINGS TO DO TODAY: Take the first step. Take one of the goals you want to achieve, and write down one step you need to take in order to obtain it. Now take that step as a goal and break it down further still – what step or steps do you need to take to achieve that? Take one of these steps and break it down further still into smaller components. Keep going until you find a mini-step that you can take TODAY.

Possible progress-preventers

As you write down your goals you may begin to identify potential obstacles – things that may prevent you from making progress and achieving your outcome. They may be real or imagined – it matters not. If you do uncover some, that's great! By spotting them now you can bring them out into the light of day and start to find solutions to overcoming them. Use your possible obstacles to create more action steps – ways through, under or around them. And if you cannot think what to do then make your goal 'to find the next step and start researching'.

Goal:

To find a hobby I really enjoy.

Possible obstacles:

1 I have no idea what I would like to do.

2 I have so little time for myself.

Steps to take:

1 Find out what I would like to do (ideas: ask a friend for ideas, read some books, look on the internet, list things I used to enjoy).

2 **Start to make time for myself (ideas: take 15 minutes every day for uninterrupted time for me; switch off the TV/computer/mobile for an hour a day).**

I suggest you keep your goal list confidential or only share it with people you trust, people who support and energise you, healthy, happy role models who believe in you unconditionally. Anyone else just might bring their own negative beliefs and energy (or lack of it) into play and may unconsciously – or even consciously – sabotage your attempts to change.

Remember, your goal list is a beginning, an exciting new start, the opening chapters to your new story. It is not the end. You are now going to require imagination, focus, self-awareness, flexibility and some keys to success. Keep reading and know that today is the day you change your life.

7

TODAY IS THE DAY YOU GET YOUR MIND TO HELP YOU

Your mind power is working, either for you or against you, from the moment you wake up in the morning to the minute you drop off back to sleep again at night (and arguably during your dreams – but that's a whole other subject).

Imagine for a moment that your thoughts are like movie directors, and your beliefs are the scriptwriters – together they create your daily mind movies, or your *imagination*. Every day at a cinema 'very close' to you, the collective creative collaboration of thoughts and beliefs are showing a daily 'experience of your world' movie. The great news is it is an interactive experience – so you can alter bits and create different endings as often as you like.

What story would you like to tell today?

Imagination doesn't have to be wild, or the sole domain of story-tellers, it is something you use all the time. When you think about the day ahead, you are imagining it. When you think about what is likely to happen with a project at work, you are imagining it. When you think about how your partner is going to react to something, you are imagining it. OK, so you may base your imaginings on things from the past, but they are still imaginings. And it this very habit of basing things on past experiences that can keep us stuck!

Think about the events, conditions and circumstances being consistently experienced in various areas of your life... then think about your predominant thoughts, what you imagine most often about those areas, and you will see a connection.

Relationships Do you imagine they are easy and satisfying? Do you imagine struggles and difficulties? Do you imagine a perfect marriage or a potential divorce?

Work Do you imagine spending every day doing something you love? Do you imagine hard work and toil? Do you imagine always doing the same thing?

Money Do you imagine abundance? Do you imagine having to work hard to make ends meet? Do you imagine not having enough at the end of the month?

The future Do you imagine achieving all you desire? Do you imagine being just like your parents? Do you imagine things going well – or things going badly?

Health Do you imagine great health and vigour? Do you imagine regenerating or degenerating? Do you imagine illness?

Fitness Do you imagine becoming and staying fitter? Do you imagine declining fitness? Do you imagine pottering or running a marathon?

Anything you create in your life begins in your mind as an image

Anything you create in your life begins in your mind as an image – be it a sandwich or a successful international business. A great way to start every day is to spend five minutes imagining your day running smoothly and perfectly. Run through the coming day's events in your mind imagining the best possible outcomes and imagine yourself at the end of the day, relaxed and satisfied. Some of my biggest doubters have initially shunned this exercise as 'wishful thinking', but having been persuaded to give it a go for a few days have been astounded by the results.

'I struggled with it for the first couple of days, but even then felt better for just having five minutes relaxing time to myself. Then it got easier and became fun imagining everything going great. My wife and the kids all said I was much happier to be around at breakfast time, which meant us all leaving the house in much better moods. Starting the day feeling good certainly made a difference, and then I started using the same technique before meetings, or on my way home from work. I just kept imagining everything going well. My colleagues asked me what I kept smiling about! I guess

there are a number of reasons why this might work, but actually I don't need to know, I just know it has made a major impact on my life.'

Don't worry, be happy

If you start the day worrying then you are doing the flip side of the above and imagining the worst rather than the best (possibly for much longer than five minutes!) – so why not switch it around and spend that time thinking about positive things instead? Worry is just about the worst form of mental activity there is. It is a waste of time and energy and does more harm than good. It can even make you ill! Doctors' waiting rooms are full of people who have 'worried-themselves-sick'. Indigestion, heart problems, insomnia, irritable bowel syndrome and backache are just a few of the symptoms experienced by habitual worriers. Why not try 'imagining yourself better' instead. There is much evidence of the power of the mind over the body – so put it to good use.

MIND OVER MOVEMENT

Stand up, feet shoulder-width apart and feeling balanced. Raise both arms in front of you until they are parallel with the floor. Now slowly turn to your left and with no pushing or straining reach as far as you comfortably can, following your fingertips with your eyes. Look at where your fingers stop and mentally mark that point in the room. Now turn back around, relax your arms down, close your eyes and imagine yourself turning again – only this time imagine turning much further, with ease. Relax. Now imagine it again – this time reaching further still; imagine feeling flexible and ▶

comfortable. Now open your eyes and repeat the first step again. Did you reach further than the first time? Congratulations – you just programmed yourself to go beyond your perceived limits.

Worry is mentally taxing, too. It creates stress, anxiety and exhaustion, for the worrier and those around him or her. Mental capacity can be affected and before long you can find yourself seemingly stuck in a downward spiral, worrying about worrying, and worrying about how dreadful you feel as a result. Worriers are prone to depression and are more likely to smoke, drink and suffer addiction in many forms.

Imagine you have two advisors: Mr Worry and Mr Reassurance. How different would they be? Which one would you rather take guidance from? Who would you rather emulate?

All in all, worry does not have a lot going for it. Of course there are likely a few of you who are addicted to this mental preoccupation and are already thinking of a few reasons to keep it up. I asked ten worry-prone people to write a list of 'good' reasons to worry. Here are a few of their responses:

'Gives me control over situations.'

'Keeps me safe.'

'Helps me solve problems.'

'Stops me making mistakes.'

'Prepares me for the worst.'

'Stops me thinking about other things.'

'Gives me something to think about.'

'It's easy – because I do it so much.'

'It's familiar.'

'Keeps me on my toes.'

Now if you read the above list as part of an advertisement you'd probably buy the product. How fantastic! Something that allows you to control situations, keeps you safe, helps you solve problems, stops you making mistakes and prepares you for the worst. Bring it on! We'd all like some of that. But *is it true*? Can 'worry' really do any of those things? And what if you read the small print on the advert? What about the side-effects?

I asked the same ten people to write a list of how worrying affects them mentally and physically. Here are some of their responses:

'I regularly get palpitations.'

'Dreadful anxiety.'

'Distress.'

'Agitation.'

'Sleeplessness.'

'Can't think straight.'

'Panic attacks.'

'Frequent headaches.'

'Upset tummy.'

'Shoulder and neck pains.'

'Aggravates my asthma and eczema.'

Do you still want to buy it?

Worry is a function of the imagination. If you couldn't imagine things, you couldn't worry. Imagination is a wonderful thing – when used to our advantage. Because we can imagine, we can plan ahead and picture different future possibilities. Imagination offers us the opportunity to steer our course through life and make decisions and choices about possible futures. So why would you want to waste such a gift imagining the worst?

Worry involves focusing on fear – what happens if you focus on the opposite?

 THINGS TO DO TODAY: Ask yourself: how do I use worry to hold myself back? What do I waste energy worrying about? What could I better use that energy for?

The great news is there is *plenty* you can do. You can learn to use your imagination consciously, effectively and skilfully. You can realise how useless and unproductive worrying is and learn to catch yourself doing it – then do something different instead. Get your mind to help you – not hinder you.

I asked ten people who use their imaginations positively to write a list of 'good' reasons to do so. Here are a few of their responses:

'Makes me feel in control, rather than a victim.'

'Sets me up for the day.'

'Helps me solve problems.'

'Feels great!'

'Changes my state.'

'Gives me more energy.'

'It's easy – because I do it so much.'

'Changes how things work out.'

'Improves my self-confidence.'

'Relaxes and calms me.'

And the side-effects?

'More energy.'

'Better sleep.'

'Generally healthier!'

'Better decision-making.'

'Calmer.'

Magic Moment Mind Movies (or Mmmm)

Think of three wonderful moments from any time in your life, from childhood to present day. Times when you felt really great. They don't have to be earth-shatteringly momentous, just times when you felt that all was well with your world (and if you cannot recall any – make some up, imagine some wonderful scenarios). Here are some examples from others that may prompt you to recall your own magic moments:

When my little boy hugs me and says 'I love you Mummy'.

Scuba diving in the Maldives.

Sitting in front of a log fire at the end of a lovely day.

Watching an amazing sunset.

Being promoted at work.

Getting my exam results – and passing!

Riding my horse for the first time.

Find your own feel-good thoughts and spend time with each one

Find your own feel-good thoughts and spend time with each one. Recall the moment as fully as you can. What could you see/hear/feel/smell? Luxuriate in the moment again and again in your mind. How good does that feel? Do this regularly with each of your chosen magic moments and then next time you find yourself playing a worry movie in your head, switch to your Magic Moments channel and watch something different instead. You will soon feel quite different.

A common theme for worriers is worrying about 'others'. In worry mode we imagine what others are thinking, feeling, doing, about to do, have done, and so on. We expend precious energy on something that only exists in our imagination. And how does that affect how we are with those others? It is a no-win situation and an exhausting one to-boot.

 THINGS TO DO TODAY: Bring awareness to your mind and your imaginings. What mind movies are you playing in your head as you wake-up/head out for the day/go to the office/go shopping/meet someone...? Become aware of how they shape your experiences. What can you do to change them?

Belief – thought – image – action

What you believe shapes your thoughts. Your thoughts create the images in your mind (though arguably those images are part of your thoughts!) and your actions are responses to these. And then there is a feedback loop, an 'I told you so' element to your thinking... so off you go again.

Here's an example:

You have a meeting at work and you **believe** meetings to be a hassle that invariably result in you having more work to do and feeling out of your depth.

This **thought** creates an **image** in your mind of you walking in late to a room full of serious faces and silence.

That **image** fills you with dread and as a result of trying to calm your nerves you do arrive a little late and have forgotten an important document.

'There, I told you so – meetings are always a hassle!'

(Belief enforced!)

Now imagine another example, starting with a different belief:

You have a meeting at work and you **believe** meetings to be a great way to share and exchange information with colleagues.

This **thought** creates an **image** in your mind of a room full of eager, welcoming faces and chatter.

That **image** fills you with keen anticipation so you arrive early and burst through the door with a smile on your face.

'There, you see – I told you so, meetings are great!'

(Belief enforced!)

The great news is that by becoming aware of what we are imagining we can change it!

By catching our beliefs and using the power of our minds to visualise (or imagine) something different we can change our thoughts, feelings and actions and gain conscious control of our lives.

More than pictures

Not everyone can 'see' vivid, photo-quality pictures in their mind – including me. I believe this is why the word visualisation can put people off because it implies a kind of inner seeing. What I (and maybe you) do experience is an awareness of something, which might involve bringing in feeling, smell, sound, taste or a combination of these. Imagine for a minute a rose. You may not create a clear image, but you will get a feeling of what a rose means to you. Maybe you smell the fragrance, imagine the vase, bouquet, or garden it is in, feel the petals (or the thorns), or hear the snip of secateurs as they prune the bush. You may not be able to see the rose clearly, but can probably tell me what colour, size and shape it is and how many blooms there are around it. And all that in an instant.

We don't all perceive the world in the same fashion, and we don't all 'imagine' in the same fashion either. Actually, about 40 per cent of the population is more sensitive to sight (visual), 30 to 40 per cent reacts more to feeling (kinaesthetic), and 20 to 30 per cent is more receptive to sound (auditory). Usually we are a little of each – with maybe one sense that predominates.

Knowing your own type/s can help you make better use of your mind power. As a largely kinaesthetic person anything based largely on visualisation is lost on me. The more someone tells me to 'picture' something, to 'see' an outcome or 'visualise' a perfect day the more frustrated and despondent I can become. And the same applies to 'visual' friends when asked to 'feel' how something is, or to imagine how they would 'feel about' something… they just can't get it!

 THINGS TO DO TODAY: Everybody has the ability to visualise or imagine, but we may all do it a little differently. How do you perceive and imagine the world? Are you predominantly auditory, visual or kinaesthetic? Think of an enjoyable place you visited a while ago. What is the first thing that comes to your mind? The way it looked, the different sounds you heard, or the feeling you had being there? This is one of the questions that can help you determine whether you are more visual, auditory or kinaesthetic.

Notice how people around you express themselves, too. Pay attention to their choice of words. Expressions such as 'It looks good to me', 'That rings a bell' or 'It doesn't quite feel right' could respectively reveal visual, auditory or kinaesthetic tendencies.

Talking to a 'visual' person using 'feeling' words can be rather like speaking a different language! Becoming aware of how you and others perceive the world can make everybody's life easier, especially yours!

'Imagination is everything – it is the preview of life's coming attractions'

There is a lovely quote from world-renowned scientist Albert Einstein: 'Imagination is everything – it is the preview of life's coming attractions.' And there are many wonderful stories to support his theory.

IMAGINARY GOLF

I remember reading about an amazing man who had been a prisoner of war. For seven years Air Force Colonel George Hall was locked in the dark box of a North Vietnamese prison. It would have been easy to crumble under such conditions – either physically or mentally. But this incredible man chose to use his mind to help him escape the horrors of his situation. He loved to play golf, so every day for seven years he chose to play a full game of golf in his imagination – a perfect 18 holes, day in, day out. I can only imagine that his imaginary daily game of golf became a wonderful place to escape to. The reports say that one week after he was released from his POW camp he entered the Greater New Orleans Open and completed the round in a score of 76. It was the best round of golf he had ever played... and this for a man who hadn't played a 'real' round for seven years – except in his imagination!!

This is an extreme example – but nevertheless it illustrates an important point for anyone wishing to change their life: the power of the mind is incalculable and way beyond the understanding of science. The human brain has been dissected, probed, examined, studied, scrutinised and tested more than perhaps any other part of the body. Yet we are still far from any definition of what we call 'the mind'.

IMAGINE YOUR GOALS

(This is a great exercise to do with a partner, but can be done alone. It is very powerful and people are regularly surprised by the changes that come as a result.)

Take six pieces of A4 paper and a thick marker pen.

On each piece of paper clearly (in large letters) write a goal you wish to achieve. Keep your writing brief – use key words – you do not need to describe the goal in great detail.

Now choose a space on the floor that represents today. Imagine a line extending from the space that represents today and decide where on that line the future is. Lay your goals out along your imaginary line – put them wherever you would wish to have achieved them in your future – for instance six months from today, one year, five years and so on.

Once all six goals are where you want them to be on your future line, I want you to step onto your first goal. Read the goal, then close your eyes and imagine it is happening right now – be there and bring it alive in your imagination (what can you see, feel, hear, smell?). Stay there for as long as you wish.

Before you go onto your next goal, turn and look back at the spot you originally marked on the floor as today. From your new place of having achieved your goal, what advice would you give to the you back then?

Do this for all six goals.

Before you leave this chapter, spend a moment imagining yourself a year from today. Look back at all you did and achieved, remember for a while those lovely times/holidays/successes. Smile as you recall the fun and the laughter. Celebrate your achievements/accomplishments/triumphs/realisations. Notice how much healthier and more energetic you feel, how much more at peace with yourself and your life. Wonder at how much those little changes added up and grew into one of the best years of your life.

Now go and enjoy it!

8
TODAY IS THE DAY YOU FOCUS ON THE LITTLE THINGS (THAT MAKE BIG THINGS HAPPEN)

Many of us are drawn to big dramatic change – it excites us, especially after another day of the same old, same old… Big change is entertaining, too; look how many TV shows are created around this theme: extreme make overs, home transformations, drastic diets, dream moves and talent shows (unemployed spinster bags million-dollar record deal). The public (that's us) love to tune in and get drawn into other people's major life changes. Wow, I could do that too! The reality, of course, is that when we try to make over our lives from top to bottom – before next week we're right back to our old ways. We are creatures of habit and struggle with too much change all at once.

I understand that when you want to change your life it can suddenly feel crucial to get EVERYTHING done right now, right away: you want to lose weight, change career, improve your relationships, get fit, improve your social life, feng shui your home… oh, and reduce stress! But attempting to change too much in one go would require super-human effort, and if you don't find yourself matching up to the exacting standards of a super hero you will probably give up.

If your 'to do' list requires first-rate time-management skills in order for you to plot a course through a daily regimen fit to test a super hero – then you probably won't see it through. Why? Because it is unrealistic, overwhelming and too much like hard work. Whatever happened to quality of life and balance?

There is good news though! Real change can happen right now without wearing yourself out in the process. In this chapter we are going to think small and make big differences. We are going to take on board the truth that small actions add up, that real change is about small adjustments practised over time, and that even a five per cent change can alter your life dramatically. If you were heading out on a boat on the ocean and at the last minute you changed your plotted course by a tiny fraction, you'd end up many miles from the destination you'd originally planned. And life is like that. Change something by even the smallest percentage and your outcomes will be different.

THINGS TO DO TODAY: Write down five small things you could do differently today that you would feel good about. Then do them!

Changing your life is not just about setting and achieving large goals, it is also about moment-to-moment tweaks and changes you can make in the small details of your everyday life: different choices and decisions you can make day by day; becoming aware of and altering your thoughts if they don't serve you; and being 'in the moment' – acknowledging and appreciating what is good 'right now'.

 THINGS TO DO TODAY: Write down ten things you appreciate about your life right now. Remind yourself of these when you wake in the morning and before you go to sleep at night.

And you don't have to give up on any grand plans either. You can dream as big as you like, but as with most successful people in life, once you know where you want to be you need to make a workable plan to get you there – with daily steps. If millionaire status is your goal and you're currently living hand to mouth, then you could start by saving, making or investing your first extra £10 today. If a fit and slim body is your goal and you are weighing in at more than your ideal weight, then you could decide that today you will leave some food on your plate at the end of every meal. Start right now by taking a measurable, simple step towards the change you desire – and the change has already begun.

Start right now by taking a measurable simple step towards the change you desire

THINGS TO DO TODAY: Write down 100 small things you could do to change your life in small but positive ways.

Examples:

Create a special place This is the place you 'always' put your keys/wallet/phone/purse – all the vitals that tend to go missing just as you are about to leave the house!

Take thankful breaks Take such breaks at times throughout your day – moments when you pause and acknowledge something that is great about your life today.

Display uplifting pieces Display pictures/photos/paintings/quotes/notes that uplift you.

Sort your mail near your recycling bin Get rid of junk mail, surplus letters and envelopes straight away. If you haven't time to sort the proper mail have a specific spot you always put that too.

Read, watch or listen to something/someone funny every day Do whatever it takes to make you laugh out loud.

Do something different

Whether you are clear about your goals or still working out exactly where you are headed, nothing will change unless you do something different. And if you are stuck in a pattern (i.e. things keep not working out and you keep doing the same things), do something different to break the pattern. For instance, if you keep arguing with your partner/colleague/child – next time the heat starts to rise adopt a different stance/sit on the floor/ balance a cup on one hand. Use your imagination with this one: any habit you wish to break, do something 'unusually' different while you go about 'it'. See what changes!

Think about your typical day. Many of us get so used to our routines we hardly ever stop to wonder whether we are doing something the best way (for us) or just because it's how we've always done it! We potentially limit ourselves. Of course there is some comfort in familiar routines, but it is worth checking-in to see if we are missing other possibilities that may expand and improve our lot. What small changes could you make to your routine today?

Buy a different newspaper.

Sit in a different seat on the train/bus/for lunch/at work.

Watch something different on TV – or NO TV for an evening.

Tune into a different radio station.

Shop in another store/s.

Only buy foods you've never bought before.

Wear a new style/colour.

Change your posture/how you walk (for the better).

Behave differently (for example: swap assertiveness for non-assertiveness, or vice versa).

Set your alarm clock for half an hour earlier than usual.

Spend time with someone different.

And you never know where doing something different might lead you… One woman enrolled herself on a yoga course for the first time – and five years later became a yoga teacher. A man went along to a meeting at a local allotment – and now grows all his family's veg, transforming their eating habits and health. One woman spent her short daily train journey writing a story – and is now a published author.

Taking that first step

Imagine five birds perching on a branch, and then one makes the decision to fly off to a magic faraway land where he believes the nectar to be of supreme quality and the birds plentiful. How many birds are left on the branch? That's right, five. One made the decision to jump off, but didn't actually 'do' anything about it. You can spend months (or years) imagining, planning, deciding and understanding what has to be done, but it is the 'doing' that will get you there.

SMALL STEPS, BIG RESULTS

Rob had been overweight since his teens. At school he had been taunted and teased, and since then had kind of grown comfortable with his size and accepted the generally-held perception that he was 'cuddly Rob' – a good friend to go eating and drinking with, but not one to invite along on any excursion requiring any degree of athleticism or fitness. However, a health scare at the tender age of 31 had shocked Rob and he realised that his acceptance of his weight was actually his way of pretending everything was OK. He was suddenly afraid, aware of his mortality and embarrassed by his size. Determined to get healthy he vowed that from that day onwards he would never again spend evenings drinking pints, all sweet and fatty foods were to be banned from his diet and he would join a gym and get lean and fit.

Day one was a relative success. He went without his usual sweet-pastry on the way to work, his lunchtime latte was swapped for herbal tea, chips were off the menu at dinner and he did not go to the pub in the evening. Hungry, and a little tense, he was nevertheless pleased with himself as he went to bed at the end of the day. The next day he was going to stop off at the local gym on the way back from work and get himself signed up.

▶

Day two started well. He managed to once again cut down on his food during the day, but *en route* to the gym his nerves got the better of him and he munched on a chocolate bar and a bag of crisps (reckoning he would soon work that off – once he joined the gym). It took Rob 15 minutes to sum up the courage to leave the safe confines of his car for the gym. 'It was like all the years I had spent pretending I was OK being overweight suddenly caught up with me, my heart was racing, my hands were sweaty and I hated myself. Summing up the courage to walk into the gym and pick up a membership form felt like one of the hardest things I had ever done. I wondered how the hell I was ever going to get in there to work out if this bit was so difficult.'

That evening Rob had a huge dinner and took himself to the pub for a pint – desperate to seek the comfort of regular friends and surroundings. By bedtime on day two Rob felt like a complete failure; he had failed to make all the changes he had promised himself he would make – all within two days. Rob became depressed, he gained more weight and his work began to suffer.

During coaching sessions to help him at work the issue of Rob's weight came up, and it was clear that his feelings of failure connected to his intended weight loss and fitness regime were affecting all areas of his life. With help Rob clarified his intention to transform his health and created a strong vision for a future fit and slim Rob. He then created a list of small steps he could take towards his goal. Going to the gym and cutting out all the 'bad foods' in one go was not an option – he had already tried that and suffered the repercussions.

Rob started small and set attainable goals that he knew he could accomplish. He swapped one snack a day to fruit or veg, walked for 20 minutes at lunchtime, drank a glass of water three times

▶

a day, put a bit less on his plate each mealtime and bought some hand weights and did some exercises while watching TV in the evening. These were all small changes to his usual daily routines and he introduced them one at a time, at his own pace. His sense of achievement motivated him daily and he never felt overwhelmed by the task ahead. Before he knew it he was feeling lighter and fitter, his friends were commenting and he really felt like it had required little effort. Small step after small step, Rob eventually joined the gym and has never looked back since.

 THINGS TO DO TODAY: Do something for five minutes. Sometimes the sheer scale of a project keeps us from getting started. Take the most manageable bite possible, and spend five minutes taking a first step, or steps, such as:

Clearing out a cupboard.

Jotting down ideas for a book.

Looking for a new job.

Exercising.

Starting a project list.

Make it a habit

Research shows that it takes 21 days to develop a habit – and it takes just one day to get started! So if you want to change something in your life (start exercising, eat healthily, meditate, wake early, get your work done on schedule… anything!), start today and then do the same for the next 20 days. That doesn't sound as daunting as committing for a lifetime does it? After 21 days new neural pathways will have formed and it will be easy to continue – and you will already be reaping the benefits. In fact, because you have established a new habit it may even be harder *not* to engage in the new behaviour than it was starting it.

 THINGS TO DO TODAY: What good habits can you start today... and continue for 21 days? List five things, such as:

Give up coffee.

Give up sweets/chocolate/biscuits.

Spend 15 minutes in relaxed silence every day.

Write in a journal.

Drink a vegetable or fruit smoothie every day.

Give yourself extra time for any journey and be on (or ahead of) time.

Put a spring in your step and smile.

Drink more water.

Take a walk at lunchtime.

Where to start?

If you have written your goal list but not got started, do it today! Choose one of your goals and ask yourself what is the easiest step I can take right now in the direction of what I want? Write down three things you can do within the next 24 hours to move you closer to your goal. And if choosing just one of your goals proves testing, then I suggest you take the biggest, most daunting one first, because without doubt 'it' will be affecting many other areas of your life. By taking a step towards a major 'biggie' you are likely to feel a sense of pride and relief – both great motivators.

CLARIFYING YOUR GOALS

Judy's big goal was to be in a job she loves one year from now as working at a job she dislikes was affecting her relationships and her health. I checked in with her two months after she first set her goal.

'Whenever I think about this goal I feel overwhelmed and not sure where to start. I hate my job but am so busy with it and worn out at the end of the day that I keep doing nothing. Also I just do not know what kind of job I do want!'

Judy recognised that the lack of clarity in her goal was making it harder for her and until she knew what kind of job she wanted she felt like she was directionless. Together we brainstormed and made a list of small steps Judy could take right away towards achieving her goal – and top of her list was:

Make my goal more specific.

This simple realisation enthused Judy to do some soul searching about what kind of work she would really love to be doing. And the best thing of all is she could start taking steps right away by asking herself some questions – something easily slotted into her busy schedule.

'I hate my job' is a phrase I regularly hear from many people, and frequently the problem is they don't actually know what job they do want. If you are stuck with a similar dilemma and would like to work out a solution, start with a few questions today:

What parts of your job do you enjoy?

What skills do you have (in any area of life)?

What job would you do if money were not part of the equation?

What do you love doing?

Are there jobs that involve doing what you love doing?

Who are you jealous of? What do they do?

What job would you apply for if you were guaranteed success?

What did you want to be 'when you grew up'?

What would you like to be remembered for?

What small adjustment can you make to your life today that will make a big difference? Here are a few ideas to help you along:

Goals to aim for	Small adjustments to make
I want to be fit.	Take 15 minutes' exercise TODAY.
	Park the car further from work.
	Get off the train/bus one stop sooner and walk.
	Use the stairs - not the lift.
	Get up and move around at work at regular intervals!
I want to be slimmer.	Eat only fruit or veg at afternoon snacktime.
	Drink a glass of water an hour before a meal.

Goals to aim for	Small adjustments to make
	Go to the shop and stock up on healthy, non-fattening snacks.
	Put a picture of a slimmer me on the fridge/cupboard door.
	Always leave something on my plate at the end of a meal.
I want to improve my relationships.	Give my partner an unexpected hug.
	Be my own best friend.
	Tell someone what I appreciate about them.
	Put myself in the other's shoes.
	Truly listen to what others are saying.
I want to gain more confidence.	List ten things I am good at.
	Walk like someone who is confident.
	Focus on something I am great at.
	Do something I have been putting off.
	Read or listen to something inspirational.

Large changes occur in tiny increments

Look-at-the-big-picture thinking runs the risk of ignoring the fact that change is based on small, small steps – that large changes occur in tiny increments. Rather than taking baby steps towards their dreams, some people rush to the edge of the cliff but then stand there quaking, saying 'I can't leap, I can't leap'. It is far better to take one small daily action than to attempt too much too soon and scare yourself. Set yourself up to succeed. Think in terms of a space flight: by altering the launch trajectory very slightly, you could end up discovering a wonderful new planet.

9

TODAY IS THE DAY YOU CHOOSE WHO YOU LISTEN TO

If you were to spend every moment of every day (and night) for the rest of your life with someone – what would you want them to be like? How would you like them to talk to you? Would you want them to be:

A – loving, supportive, encouraging, empowering and fun?

or

B – critical, unsupportive, negative and miserable?

It's a no-brainer really, isn't it?

And if you were unfortunate enough to have B around, how might that affect all your other relationships as well? Would people stick around? Or rather, would the kind of people you'd really like to be with stick around? Imagine taking B along to work, parties, family-dos and socials. He or she wouldn't make you very popular.

Now imagine having A along all the time. What fun. People would be happy to see you wherever you went – and if they weren't, you wouldn't mind too much anyway because you've got A with you. Work would be easier, the party invites would probably increase and family-dos would be as you dreamed they could be. What a top companion!

Well the great news is you get to choose! Who *do* you spend more time with in your life than anyone else? Who *do* you listen to the most?

Yes – it's YOU. And it's up to you whether you fall into the A or B category. The trouble is that most of us have got so used to the sound of our own internal voices that we are hardly aware of them – yet, like having A or B along to a party, they do impact on our daily lives. Imagine tuning your personal stereo into a thoroughly miserable channel and having it play quietly in your ear all day. Now imagine tuning into an upbeat and positive channel and having that on in the background as you went about your day.

Some people struggle with the concept of voices in their heads (it sounds a little too unbalanced and whacky), so you may want to switch to thinking of them as thoughts (or self-talk). And if you are unsure how many thoughts you have per day the research does vary a little, from 12,000 to 63,000. It is also said that 90 per cent of our thoughts are repetitive, 90 per cent are about the past or the future, and a staggering 80 per cent are negative. It's a wonder any of us remain sane!

Self-talk is the running dialogue that goes on inside your head. Even if you are not aware of it, we all have it. Patterns of negative or positive self-talk often start in childhood. Your self-talk will have coloured your thinking for years, and affected you in many ways. However, any time can be a good time to change it! At this moment your self-talk is the words you are reading, but if you stop reading for a moment you may think 'I know what self-talk is so I don't need to read this bit', or 'oh my goodness, she has a point here'. Or your self-talk may do its best to distract you from reading – in which case we may be hitting on a nerve and my suggestion would be to carry on reading!

Who's in charge?

The majority of people do not control their thoughts, but they allow their thoughts to control them… for instance, if you regularly speak negatively to yourself you will attract a host of other negative thoughts. As a result of these negative thoughts you will experience negative feelings – and these will probably lead to negative actions… and so the cycle continues. However, any suggestion that you can control all your thoughts from here on in, or any suggestion that if you cannot then you have failed, is nonsense. The most powerful thing you can do *today* is to raise your awareness about your own thoughts. You probably don't realise how often you say negative things in your head, or how much it

The most powerful thing you can do *today* is raise your awareness about your own thoughts

affects your experience of life. The second most powerful thing you can do is to become detached from those thoughts, be an observer – maybe even laugh a little. Awareness can be curative.

 THINGS TO DO TODAY: Conduct some self-talk research. Pay attention today to your thoughts, to the way you talk to yourself internally. Don't try and change anything, for now just take your awareness to what you are thinking. Are your thoughts predominantly negative or positive? Are they about the past, the future or the now? Are there patterns? When your mind wanders, where does it go? What do you think about? Maybe have a notebook to hand and jot down some thoughts as they come up – without editing!

If all this mention of self-talk and research and positive and negative thoughts leaves you thinking, 'what a lot of...', then let me ask you a few questions:

How does that thought serve you? What feeling does it evoke and what action will it precede? Will it help you make the changes in your life you wish for?

Call to your mind the happiest person you know – what do you imagine their self-talk is like?

Call to mind the most miserable person you know – what do you imagine their self-talk is like?

Call to mind the most successful person you know – what do you imagine their self-talk is like?

Call to mind the most unsuccessful person you know – what do you imagine their self-talk is like?

Convinced?

Turning thoughts into actions

Thought alone will not change your life – it has to produce action

Buddha taught: all that we are is the result of what we have thought. And countless other spiritual and self-development teachers of every persuasion and belief have been sharing a similar message with us since time began – so we are in good company here.

However, thought alone will not change your life – it has to produce action (small action is fine, remember small actions add up).

EMPTY DREAMS

A friend of mine went on what was billed as a 'life-changing weekend'. The literature promised all sorts of wonderful things – including help in achieving the life he desired and mastering his home and work life. It also cost a lot of money – surely a sign that it must be good! He spent two days being pumped-up to a state of high excitement. He chanted and cheered along with the others as they all wove extraordinary dreams and saw themselves succeeding beyond all previously conceived expectations. He came back a changed man – for about two days. By day three he was actually quite low. 'I felt so let down; nothing had changed, in fact things felt worse because I now felt like a failure – one with £2,000 less in the bank!', he explained. It seemed the course had missed out on a vital ingredient: action. Yes, thoughts are incredibly powerful things – but unless they prompt a change in what you are doing, nothing will change. My friend had been encouraged to dream big, but he had not had the opportunity to identify the steps required to reach his destination. It now all seemed like a lot of wild, crazy unobtainable dreams. He did nothing different – and 'thought' of himself as a failure.

If you already think that the idea of voices in your head is slightly crazy – then the idea that you might give them characters may be stretching things a little... but bear with me.

Let's take my aforementioned friend as an example. Through years and years of programming, there resided in his head a Mr Discouraging. If ever he attempted to step outside his comfort zone, Mr D would pipe up and urge him to 'not be so daft'. He would warn him of everything that could possibly go wrong, remind him how someone with his upbringing would never make it anywhere special in life and tell him what a fool he would likely make of himself if he tried. Enough to stop most people in their tracks!

Now Mr D actually had good intentions – he wanted to keep my friend safe, help him avoid humiliation and let-down – but in doing so he prevented him from experiencing many new and wonderful things in his life. He had looked after him since childhood and was not going to be easily dissuaded from continuing along the way he had always known.

Alongside Mr D there lives Mr Encouraging, but he is far less practised and powerful. He is generally shouted down by Mr D and has become progressively afraid of having his say. He loved the weekend away on the workshop; he came out of hiding and puffed himself up to mega proportions. For two whole days Mr D hardly got a look in – and he was not happy about that. He listened to Mr E encourage my friend to do all sorts of amazing things and together they created a dream-like future vision. Mr D tried to pipe up, but the cacophony of encouraging voices drowned him out for once.

However, he bided his time and within 48 hours of the three of them being back on home ground he was able to make himself heard once again – only now he was angry (and afraid) and had a whole weekend's worth of pent-up discouragement to vent! There was little wonder my friend suddenly felt so low.

Mr D isn't all bad though. He would secretly like to change, but he is comfortable in his discomfort and afraid that any change might actually be for the worst. He requires a gentle hand, and a steady-steady approach. It's no good telling him there is a pot of gold at the end of the rainbow but not showing him how to get to it. He needs to take baby steps, to stick his toe in the water and make sure it is safe. He can change, but he needs help.

It is claimed that between only five and ten per cent of our daily conscious thoughts are new ones… meaning that most of them are habitual. In the above example Mr D occupies the 90 to 95 per cent slot – so he has a firm foothold. But he *can* change. With will-power and attention we can all introduce new thoughts into our minds and – most importantly – take action on them. Habits can be broken – and new ones introduced.

Negative to positive

Once you're aware of your internal dialogue you can work on ways to change it. Listen to the words you use when things are not going to plan. For instance, instead of using strong emotive words such as 'hate' and 'useless' ('I hate writing reports, I am useless at them'), you could use milder words such as 'don't like' and 'not great' ('I don't like writing reports, I am not great at them') – they sound so much gentler and less likely to knock you off centre. And if you find yourself complaining about something, stop and look for the positive – for instance, if you have just had a meeting cancelled at the last minute, then rather than saying 'I don't believe it, what a waste of time, and now I am behind on…', you could say 'So what can I do with this new unexpected free time?'

The next time you are feeling stressed or anxious about something, see what you can say to yourself to help change your perspective. And play close attention to self-limiting statements such as 'I can't handle this', 'This is impossible' or 'I don't stand a chance'. Swap them instead for questions: 'How can I handle this?', 'How can I make this possible?' or 'What is the best thing I can do in this situation?'

THINGS TO DO TODAY: If you are having difficulty listening-in to your internal chatter – pay attention to what you say out loud about yourself (it will give you clues). You could even ask a trusted friend/colleague/partner to tell you what negative messages they hear you give to yourself repeatedly. Here are some examples of external negative self-talk:

'I can never remember people's names.'

'I am so stupid.'

'I always get lost.'

'I usually say the wrong thing.'

'I'm just not lucky.'

'Things always go wrong for me.'

Listen-in

And there's another voice you can listen to – your 'inner voice' or intuition. If mind-chatter comes from your head, then intuition can certainly feel like it comes from your gut and is often referred to as a 'gut feeling'. Intuition, sixth sense, super-conscious, insight, a hunch, gut feeling – whatever you call it, it is the ability we all have to just 'know' about a situation, a person or a decision. A knowing without knowing why.

A lot of successful business people, investors and entrepreneurs admit to using their intuition – sometimes above their logic! They have learnt to trust their gut feelings and go ahead with things

Intuition can be your greatest ally

that do not always appear 'sound and sensible', and likewise to pull things that appear to add up but just don't feel right. Provided you learn to pay attention, intuition can be your greatest ally.

When was the last time you had a hunch or feeling about something? Did you follow it or ignore it? Have you ever thought about someone just before they called you on the phone? Do you notice meaningful coincidences happening in your life? Do you pick up the feeling of a building or room? Do you get momentary thoughts that seem to come from nowhere?

Every one of us is born with the capacity for intuition, but often we partly lose it along the way. It is certainly not given much prominence in schools, universities or workplaces. But you can learn to listen.

YES OR NO?

I want you to ask yourself some questions that you absolutely know the answers to. The first set of questions is to be questions to which your answer is undeniably a YES. The second set is to be questions where the answer is an unequivocal NO.

Take a deep breath and relax before each question and physically shake yourself or move yourself between questions – so the feelings that come with your answer are in no way mixed up with the residual feelings from the previous answer. Note after each question how the YES or NO feels in your body. By doing this you are learning to tune-in to answers that come from anywhere but your mind. Your mind could lie and answer 'yes' to a 'no' question and vice versa, but you will *know* the true answer. Get familiar with your yes and no responses – they will help you tune-in to your intuition.

Here are some examples (you can make up your own or use these):

YES questions
Is my name ....(insert your own name here)....?
Do I live at ....(insert your address here)....?
Do I love ....(insert most obvious name or names here)....?

▶

NO questions

Is my name ....(insert someone else's name here)....?

Do I live on the moon?

Do I love ....(insert most unlikely name here!)....?

You are going to be spending a lot of time with yourself for the rest of your life, so if you truly wish to change your life, begin to pay attention to what you are saying to you on a daily basis. Be your own best friend and cheerleader. And when you're not so nice to be with, learn to laugh and move on.

10

TODAY IS THE DAY YOU LEAVE THE PAST BEHIND

Have you ever bungee-jumped over a ravine? Jumped from an aeroplane at 4,500ft? Skied down a glacier? White-water rafted down rapids? If you have then you will understand that part of the appeal of such extreme sports is that they force you to focus exclusively on the present moment. Part of the thrill of risking your neck 'for fun' is the intensely alive state it creates – a feeling of timelessness, leaving no space for preoccupations with the past or the future.

The good news is you do not have to go to such fast-track, extreme measures to live in the present; you can begin to make peace with your past today and you can shift your focus from past to present right now! Making peace with your past can bring you untold freedom, energy, health and happiness. When you disentangle your energy and attention from what has gone before you are suddenly able to fully engage with your life NOW – leaving you open to new opportunities and experiences.

> **Making peace with your past can bring untold freedom, energy, health and happiness**

Past life

Sometimes our preoccupation with the past is not obvious – we may not actively be seeking to recall and remember it, but our reactions and feelings today can have roots that reach way back. For instance, many people go about their daily lives feeling some degree of fear – whether it is to do with relationships, work, health, money… or fear of change. And unless the fear is a fact (for instance, you *really are* standing right in front of a charging elephant), it is a creation of the mind – a reference to something from the past.

You are afraid to date again because the last relationship ended in such pain.

You are afraid to go for promotion because you didn't get it last time.

You are afraid to stop working so hard because you/your parents once struggled for money.

You are afraid to marry because your parents divorced.

You are afraid to speak up, because last time you got shot down in flames.

Fear is always reminding you of something that happened before, warning you not to make the same mistake, cautioning you against upsetting the status quo and risking a repeat of past pain. Some see it as an aid to safety (and yes it can be useful if it gets you to move out of the path of that charging elephant) – but it is better regarded as a hindrance to happiness. Fear keeps you stuck, and if change is what you want then it's time to recognise fear for what it usually is: Fantasy Experienced As Real.

Your past will keep you stuck for as long as you allow it to – and the length of time you hold onto it is probably someway equal to the amount of fear or pain you are choosing to hold onto.

Imagine hitting your thumb really hard with a hammer – so hard that you chipped the bone, split the skin, bled and almost passed out with the pain. OUCH! Now imagine doing it again and again and again and again and again. Go on, keep hitting that thumb. Ouch, ouch, OUCH!!! How crazy is that? Well that is what we do with our minds all the time when we choose to relive painful memories – we imagine them again and again and again… and each time we feel the hurt and the pain. WHY?! You only hit your thumb the once – so why keep repeating it in your mind? It's OK to acknowledge your pain, but you do not have to keep reliving it in detail.

It's OK to acknowledge your pain

THINGS TO DO TODAY: You can't change the things that have happened in your life, but you can decide how you interpret and respond to them. Do you feel you lacked support in the past when you needed it? What kind of support would you have liked to receive? Give it to yourself now.

Holding onto the past can be addictive. And like many addictions you may not be aware you 'have it'. Ask yourself – how many DO you have a day? How many times do you think about the past? Do you just find yourself thinking about the past without realising you are doing it? How soon after you wake in the morning are you reaching for an old memory? Do you just have to have one more before you go to bed at night?

Like any addiction it is no good anyone else telling you to drop it – you've got to want to do this for yourself. Ask yourself: does your thinking about the past empower you or disempower you? Does your reliving of the past keep you stuck? Can you imagine what effect dropping your addiction to your past would have on your relationships/work/life in general? Would you rather be saying 'YES' to life than 'Yes… but'? Would you like a clean slate? Do you want change for the better, or more of the same old, same old?

Moving on

Of course things do happen in life that cause pain and distress and it is important that emotions are felt and healed in an appropriate way. If you are stuck with strong feelings from your past be honest about how you feel and seek help and support. Emotions are our own personal messengers and it is important we pay them the attention they deserve if we are to grow and move forwards. Beware the misuse of positive thinking! Deep emotions cannot just be thought away or drowned out by positive affirmations and mantras. There is a saying, 'what you resist persists' – and this is certainly true of feelings that are put on hold.

Of course we can also be addicted to good and happy memories. And though these may be a whole lot pleasanter to replay, they can still prevent you from moving forward in life and embracing change. If you were blessed with wonderful good fortune in the past, beware you do not use it as a benchmark for everything in the present, dismissing everything else as 'not good enough'. Such an attitude could mean your missing out on a different kind of good fortune right now. If all your relationships are compared to a rosy glow from the past you may fail to see something very special right before your eyes. And if you turn down new avenues for work because they don't match up to a 'better' position in the past, you may just miss a pathway to a true vocation.

LETTING GO OF THE PAST

Lisa had a troubled childhood, dropped out of college, had a brush with the law, went through two acrimonious divorces and spent six months living in a hostel. 'Whenever I tried to get on with my life I felt weighed down with baggage from my past and just got angry at people because they didn't understand how bad it had been for me.'

After years of counselling she was feeling little better and embarked on a whirlwind tour of workshops, seminars, courses and retreats to help rid herself of her past. She read book after book, wrote page after page in her journals, screamed, sang, chanted, danced, cried and ate some really weird stuff. But still it was there – her past just didn't want to go.

Then one day, sitting at a bus stop, she got talking to an elderly lady who was loaded down with shopping bags. Lisa did her usual thing and told the lady her life story; told her how no one understood, how she was broke after spending so much money on

▶

courses that hadn't worked and how she wished her life could have been different. The lady listened and nodded. Lisa helped her onto the bus with her bags and talked some more. The lady stood up ready to get off at her stop and turned to Lisa. 'My Dear', she said, 'You are wasting your wishes on the past, you cannot change that and you need to accept that. Use your wishes for the future; there is still a very good chance that you can change that.' And with that she got off the bus – without her shopping. Lisa managed to quickly get the driver to stop the bus and she called down the road to tell the lady she had forgotten her bags, but she couldn't see her.

'That day changed my life more than any other before', explained Lisa. 'All the things I had tried in order to somehow change my past or forget, and it took one old lady on a bus to wake me up. All it took was someone pointing out that I couldn't change my past but could change my future. It was like a light-bulb going on in my head. I have been back to the bus stop a few times hoping to meet her again and thank her but she is never there. Sometimes I think she wasn't real – she must have been an angel or something. Yet it was her very realness that made me listen. It was strange how she left her shopping bags behind too, it felt symbolic.'

The past is passed. You wouldn't drive with most or all of your focus on the rearview mirror (at least not for long!) – so why do it in life? You cannot change the past and accepting that is one of the greatest gifts you can give to yourself. We all have a story. We all have a history and may wish we could rewrite our scripts and have a memory full of picture-perfect times, but we can't. You may have regrets, guilt, wish you'd treated someone differently and wish to wipe the slate clean, but you can't. What you can do is learn from the past and make changes now – for the future. Put simply: you have a choice.

Kids from poor backgrounds get rich, and kids from rich backgrounds get poor. Kids from broken homes create happy families, and kids from happy families create broken homes. The future is not all dependent on where you came from; it is dependent on your thinking about where you came from and what you do with it in the present. Remember your thoughts are just that: your thoughts – you get to choose them. Make it your goal to learn from your past, rather than to wallow in it and allow it to cast a shadow over your present.

 THINGS TO DO TODAY: What is holding you back and preventing you from making positive changes? It will probably be something so familiar to you that you may not even recognise it at first. Try filling in the blanks to help you: 'I am afraid of . . . . because in the past . . . .'. By becoming aware that the feeling of fear you are experiencing in the present is created through your thinking, rather than your reality, you can allow yourself to choose a more empowering thought. For some people this will be a truly 'aha' moment, for others it will take time and practice and baby steps to make changes.

Focus on the good things

Have you ever noticed how things look different depending on your mood? How you can feel quite different about someone or something (past or present) after a 'good' or 'bad' day at work? Past, present and future are constantly rewriting themselves in our heads, dependent on what we are focusing on. If I am remembering things from my past in victim mode then suddenly my present and future seem full of perpetrators and pitfalls and I feel afraid. If I am feeling low today, my past suddenly becomes a series of unhappy events and my future looks desolate. When life is going well my past becomes a wonderful journey that brought me to this place and my future feels like an adventure. It all depends on where my focus is.

BE ON FOCUS ALERT!

Learn to catch yourself when your mind wanders down memory lane, or off into future fields. Are the thoughts you are having helpful and empowering? Do they make you feel good? If yes, then linger there a while and then bring those positive feelings back to the present. If your thoughts are negative and disempowering ask yourself: what can I learn from this? How is this line of thought benefiting me? Grab the lesson and get back to the here and now. Recognise how your thoughts of past and future affect your present. Find a keyword, a funny image or a sound that you can use to call yourself back and repeat it to yourself each time your mind wanders away from the present. Find one that makes you chuckle so you arrive back with a smile.

The importance of forgiveness

Making peace with your past may require you to exercise some forgiveness. But who needs to be forgiven? Many people struggle with the idea of forgiveness, reckoning that it somehow means they are approving of what happened, but this is not the case at all. Whether someone wronged you or you made a decision you regret, forgiveness is *what you do for yourself*, not for other people. When you forgive it doesn't mean that you approve of what's happened, it means that you're giving yourself permission to move on with your life.

When you forgive, you're giving yourself permission to move on with your life

Forgiveness is primarily for YOU. Yes, it is wonderful for 'the other' in the instances when you are able to turn around and say 'I forgive you' – but even that does not mean they forgive themselves! The only person you can guarantee to help by forgiving is you.

Not forgiving ought to carry a public health warning: IT CAN SERIOUSLY DAMAGE YOUR HEALTH.

Physical health – holding on to grievances, anger and resentment is bad for your physical health.

Emotional health – holding onto grievances, anger and resentment is bad for your emotional health (which in turn is bad for your physical health).

Mental health – holding onto grievances, anger and resentment is bad for your mental health (which in turn is bad for your emotional and physical health).

Relationship health – holding onto grievances, anger and resentment has a negative impact on all your relationships.

REPLAYING THE PAIN

Mark's wife of five years had left him for another man. Every morning he woke feeling angry and resentful. During each day he would picture her in his mind and remember how she had cheated on him and he would feel himself boiling over inside. At night he would lie awake imagining her being happy with the other man and his anger would keep him awake. He snapped at work colleagues (especially female ones) and fell out with his parents after they suggested he ought to 'move on'.

The idea of forgiving her seemed impossible to him. How could he? She had lied and cheated on him. She had deceived and used

▶

him. He felt that forgiving her would be like saying it was OK for someone to be dishonest and unfaithful. He felt that forgiving her would be like saying it was OK for her to cause him so much hurt and pain.

I asked Mark who was suffering most. Him or his ex? He was very clear it was him! I asked him who was causing his daily suffering? Her of course! I challenged him on this point – his wife had left him a year ago and of course he had experienced much hurt and pain, but was she really responsible for the repeated pain he was now experiencing day in and day out?

After some time Mark began to realise that it was his replaying of things over and over in his mind (many of them imagined!) that were actually harming him now. As he achieved this realisation he used a phrase that was to become his salvation: 'I wish I could just drop these thoughts'. As he said it his face became softer, and for the first time in half an hour he sat back in his chair and took a deep breath.

For Mark the idea of 'dropping it' was easier than the idea of 'forgiving' – but the outcome was the same. Together we created some magic mind movies (empowering thoughts that created feelings of calm, peace and happiness) for him to use every time he felt himself dwelling on the past in a negative way. He gave himself permission to move on with his life.

If you are struggling with forgiving someone, maybe changing your thinking about them will help. Sometimes looking at things from another viewpoint can help us to shift some stuck feelings – including putting ourselves in the other's shoes. And how different would you feel if you knew:

They had taken on a job/role/position for which they were unprepared.

They had received no help themselves.

They had little or no self-love.

They were doing their best because they had no experience of how to do it better.

They were carrying their own wounds from their own past.

They were unhappy/confused/out of their depth/afraid/unsure/hurting.

Remember, forgiveness does not mean saying it was OK or being a pushover – forgiveness means setting yourself free. By constantly reliving the pain of what happened you are giving your power away to the person who wronged you. Reclaim your power and allow yourself to move forward in life. You cannot change your past – but you can change your thinking about it.

11

TODAY IS THE DAY YOU DISCOVER THE KEYS TO SUCCESS

OK, so you know what you don't want and you know what you do want – so what's stopping you? Every year a large percentage of the population make New Year resolutions – and every year 'a large percentage' of the population break them. Thousands of people write goal lists, but far fewer actually achieve their goals. Millions embark upon diets... and, well you get the picture. Now before you shut the book in a fit of despair and give up all hope of change, STOP!! I am going to provide you with the secrets of the successful – secrets you can put to use right now.

If you want to make a change then the first key to success is to know who is responsible for your life; to know who's in the driving seat, who makes all the choices and decisions, who sometimes stands in the way, and other times motivates you? Once you know who is accountable you can turn to them for help. This person is the key to any change you wish to make, be it small or large – you cannot do it without them.

Number one key to success: You

This is your life, and how it goes (success or not) is ultimately down to you – not the 'others'. 'What!?', I hear you exclaim, 'Of course it's about him/her/them... if he/she/they would only... they are preventing me from... it's his/her/their fault we are in this mess... if he/she/they would just change... it's the system/the government/the authorities/my employers/the media...'

I know it can be a hard truth to grasp, but there is only one person you can change and that is YOU. If the above statements of blame rang true then you've probably already exhausted yourself trying to change 'the others' and become more and more exasperated in the process. However, there is a kind of magic that takes place when you start to change you – the world around you suddenly becomes different too. Remember, we don't see the world for what it is – we see the world as we are (if you're feeling miserable, then the world looks miserable, if you're feeling on top of the world, then the world looks rosy).

THINGS TO DO TODAY: Accept responsibility for your life. Spend a few moments reflecting on where you are at in life right now and acknowledge how everything is 'as it is' because of choices/decisions/actions you have made. Highlight one thing in your mind that you feel unhappy about and accept your part in creating it. This can seem a little difficult if you feel circumstances/people/jobs have shaped your life a certain way – but if you can truly accept that *you* have chosen to stay in that circumstance/relationship/job then you begin to reclaim your power. When you accept responsibility for your life as it is now, then you accept the possibility of change.

Number two key to success: The others!

Taking responsibility for your life does not mean going it alone. The human species is not designed to live in isolation. Apart from a few who maybe seek isolation for some higher spiritual goal, the majority of us thrive on company and support. High achievers in all areas of life may stand alone on the podium or platform,

High achievers have an amazing support network behind them

but you can be sure that they all have an amazing support network or team behind them. However, when looking for support be selective and seek variety. For instance, Mums are usually great for cheering you on and telling you how great you are doing – but they may sometimes lack the ability to be detached and give you honest feedback.

Seek support to help you through the change, especially if it's a big one. Big life changes can be overwhelming if faced alone, and enough of the right kind of support can make a seemingly difficult change relatively easy. If you are used to going it alone then asking for and accepting help from others may be difficult at first, but once you get used to it you'll wonder why you waited so long!

CREATE YOUR VERY OWN CHAMPIONS FOR CHANGE TEAM

Start by listing all the qualities you require from others who are to support you through change. A few examples might be:

I want people who are:

Encouraging

Inspiring

Challenging

Honest

Confidential and trustworthy

Caring

Now take some time reflecting on who is in your life and match them against the list of required qualities. For example:

Encouraging – Mum

Inspiring – Jane from Sales

Challenging – my partner

Honest – my brother

Confidential and trustworthy – my best friend

Caring – Auntie Susan

If you can't find the people to match the qualities, then you may need ▶

to think 'out of the box'. Is there someone you have overlooked because you are maybe a little afraid to ask? Someone you have lost touch with but would like to regain contact with? How about hiring a coach or counsellor? Can you think of anyone in the world who has that quality in spades and then imagine what advice or support they may give?

However you do it, build your team carefully and use them wisely. Share your hopes and dreams – that way you are more likely to put things into action. Also, be prepared to give back – to be in someone else's team and recognise the importance of such a role. It can be life-changing!

Success key number three: Know that nerves are normal

The more overactive and imaginative your mind, the more likely you are to feel nervous or afraid. Everyone gets nervous – even the most successful people on the planet – but not everyone lets their nerves get the better of them. It is worth recognising that excitement and fear create many of the same internal feelings – the thoughts that accompany them are what make the difference. Taking a bungee jump and jumping off a cliff would probably create the same physical feelings – but your experience of them would be quite different! If you are thinking of making a major change in your life you are likely to experience some nerves – even fear (or excitement!). Take this as a sign that you are leaving your comfort zone for a while and truly making a change that is worthwhile – it won't last. There's a lovely saying: 'fear is in the waiting room'... so the longer you dwell there the longer you may feel it.

Feeling nervous is normal. Allowing your mind to go into overdrive and imagining all the worst possible scenarios and outcomes, the potential major disasters and downfalls, is not very helpful! Treat your nerves as a friend, one who is concerned for your safety, sanity and wellbeing. This friend wishes to protect you, so if they have good advice take it, but only deal with the reality of what they are alerting you to – don't get caught up in their tales of doom and gloom. Nerves have a role to play in helping us to prepare for things, but recognise the difference between the real things and those prompted by your own vivid imagination. Make friends with your nerves. Thank them for wanting to protect you. Then look to other resources within you to help you do whatever it is you want to do.

 THINGS TO DO TODAY: Think of something you would like to do but are nervous of doing; something that starts jangling your nerves just by thinking about it. It can be a real goal or a wild dream (of course wild dreams can be REAL goals too!). Feeling some familiar nervous feelings already? Take a deep relaxing breath and thank the part of you that created those nerves, thank it for wanting to protect you, but tell it you have other more resourceful parts of you that can take over from here on. Now just allow an image of you doing 'whatever it is' successfully to emerge on the screen of your mind. See yourself doing it perfectly, feel the thrill of success, hear the approval of others – make your image as colourful, large and real as possible. Step into that successful you and feel the glow of achievement.

Success key number four: If at first they don't succeed – they go again, and again

When you were a baby you probably had many attempts at crawling before you finally mastered it. And when you were a toddler walking practice probably took up much of your day and you would have spent much of your time falling over. But you did it! You learnt to walk, you didn't give up, you didn't think 'oh damn, down I go again, I am no good at this, I'll never make a walker'. What's the difference today?

People who make successful changes in their lives have the courage to be imperfect

The difference is in the thinking. As an adult we can become preoccupied with what others might think and we create amazingly complex scenarios in our imaginations – enough to scare the hardiest souls from having another go. People who make successful changes in their lives have the courage to be imperfect – dare you?

Bring back some of that childlike wonder at trying things out, at wanting to learn and laughing along the way. Know that all the people whose opinions you are concerned about have a myriad of other things in their lives too and probably give far less attention to your perceived failures than you imagine. Indeed most people cheer those who continue on their path despite adversity, and those who don't have their own problems – their negativity is really nothing to do with you. If you wait to do anything till you are perfect at it, you'll never start. How can you hope to be perfect till you begin to practise? Perfect procrastination is like a swamp – it keeps you stuck.

Success key number five: Commitment

So you want to lose weight/change job/sort out a relationship/get fit/sort your finances out... whatever it is you intend to change, nothing is going to happen unless you are truly committed. And if you are not fully committed then maybe a) you are allowing fears to run the show or b) maybe you don't really want it after all, or there is something you want more than 'it' right at this moment.

For instance, many people wish to lose weight but their desire to eat comforting foods wins out. Numerous people talk about changing their jobs, but their desire to stay safe keeps them where they are. The long-term aim to become more financially prosperous may be constantly thwarted by the short-term desire to overspend for instant gratification.

Check out where you are saying one thing and doing another. What is your motivation? What do you really want? Check out the changes you say you want and score yourself from 1–10, where 1 equals 'I am not at all committed' and 10 equals 'I am fully 100 per cent committed'. If you score any less than a 10 then you need to ask yourself some questions:

Do I really want this?

What am I afraid of?

How am I stopping myself?

What is getting in the way?

What do I have to do to change my score upwards by one point... then one more... and one more?

How can I meet my need for comfort/safety/short-term gratification in a way that will empower me rather than un-power me?

What do I need first, before I can get to my goal?

Debbie Ford, in her book *The Right Questions*[1], uses a great exercise to uncover what she calls our 'underlying commitments'. To find your underlying commitments, write down a goal or desire that you've been unable to attain. Then make a list of all the actions you have taken or not taken in the past year that are in direct opposition to this goal. Now take your list and imagine that the choices that have taken you away from your desired goal or not brought you any closer to it are an expression of a

[1] Ford, D. (2003) The Right Questions: *Ten Essential Questions To Guide You To An Extraordinary Life*, Hodder Mobius, Hodder & Stoughton.

deeper commitment, your first commitment. Next, close your eyes and ask yourself, 'What commitment are these choices in direct alignment with?' There you will discover your underlying commitment.

Success key number six: Focus

It's been said a few times already – by me and many others – but we get what we focus on. Successful people know this and use it to their advantage. This doesn't mean they are perfect and always focus on the positive, but it does mean they are self-aware enough to recognise when their mood and focus shifts, and they are adept at realigning it.

Then there are the future-focused extremists. They are always aiming for the big hit of the end result. They are so focused on their future goal they could stumble over a pot of gold and not notice it. It's great to have goals, but it's also great to know how to bring yourself back into the here and now. Enjoy being grounded in the present day – and you're more likely to get what you want in the future too.

 THINGS TO DO TODAY: If you find you are not making the changes you want in life, it's most likely because you are wasting time focusing on other things. Ask yourself: 'What are the three most important things I could do today that will help me make the change/s I desire?' (All the other stuff can wait or slot in around them.)

Success key number seven: Courage

Ask yourself which is scarier: staying as you are, or making a change? Now imagine yourself ten years from now having successfully made the change and ask that future you, how would it have been if you had done nothing different? Scarier than making the change proved to be?

People who make successful changes (even if it takes them many attempts) have done their mental maths. They have identified the cost of not making the change and compared it to the cost benefit of making the change. Not making the change is costing them dearer.

Courage isn't about the absence of fear

Courage isn't about the absence of fear – it is about confronting it and going on regardless.

THINGS TO DO TODAY: Imagine two of you: the you of today and the you of the future. Now imagine the 'two of you' either side of a barrier that represents a change in your life (think of a big change you want to make and create a barrier in your mind that somehow represents it). The you of today has the barrier ahead, and the you of the future has it behind them – having successfully made the change and moved forward. Now I want both of you to face the barrier. Would the you of today like to find the courage to get to the other side? And what about the future you – would they like to come back through the barrier to the past? If you were both invited to swap sides, who would hold on tightest to what they've got?

Success key number eight: Start where you are

If you dream of running a marathon yet have not so far jogged a step, then it would be pointless going gung-ho and buying a pair of top-of-the-range running shoes and signing up for the race a couple of weeks before the date. Some things require practice and training. And it is important to start 'where you are'. A non-runner setting their goals too high is likely to either bottle-out or get hurt.

Dreams can be made real, but they tend to require realism to achieve them. You have to do something and if that something is way out of your reach you risk putting yourself off and dropping the dream. Begin at the beginning and take small, regular steps. Like the marathon runner-to-be, the first few may prove a little difficult, but after a while the going will get easier and you'll find yourself running along towards the finish line.

STEP BY STEP

Think of something you wish to achieve and write it down at the top of a sheet of paper – that is the future. Now go to the bottom of the piece of paper and write 'today'. Above the word today write one thing you could do right now as a step towards that future goal. Then above that write down the next step, and then the next, and so on – all the way to the top of the page. See how by starting where you are you can get to where you want to be; map it out and follow your plan.

12
TODAY IS THE FIRST DAY OF A WHOLE NEW LIFE

You know what you want – and what you don't want. You have set goals and made steps to reach them. You have a better understanding of the power of your mind and your self-talk. You have made a start and know how to overcome hurdles along the way. You have made every day a day to change your life.

You choose

Today is another new start – and it is up to you what you do with it. Whatever your circumstances, whatever is happening around you, you have choices: choices about what to do, and what not to do; choices about how to react, or not; choices about what to think, imagine and say to yourself; choices about how you feel and how to treat yourself. This is your life!

This is your life!

If you hear yourself starting to react with statements about 'others':

'But my boss…'

'But my partner…'

'But my kids…'

(If I offered you a first class ticket to paradise, would you still say 'Yes, but…'?)

STOP!

Recognise what you are doing. You are thinking about something that is gone and imagining how someone else is thinking and feeling based upon the past (any time from last minute to last year and beyond). Drop it and move on. Today is a new day. Make the only change you can with regard to 'others': *change how you are with them* – NOW. The past exists only in your thinking and only for as long as you choose to hang on to it. Liberate yourself today. At work or at home – you don't have to be how others expect you to be, you don't have to live 'up to' other people's expectations. If you have an issue with a colleague/friend/family member, take control and take the lead by making a change. You are your own master of change.

 THINGS TO DO TODAY: What quality can you bring to the fore to help you today? It's a new day and you get to choose: empathy, courage, humour, creativity, independence, sincerity, enthusiasm, confidence, flexibility, leadership, sensitivity, understanding, determination... pick one and use it! If you choose one that is unfamiliar to you act 'as if' you have it and see what happens.

Imagine you have a pair of magic glasses – whenever you put them on you can see clearly what is behind other people's behaviour. How different would you be if you understood that whatever anyone else says or does, it is not personal to you? The man who bumped into you out on the street – he's struggling with addiction. The woman who stole your parking spot – she's going through a divorce. The guy who pushed in to the front of the queue – his child is in hospital. The man who let the door go in your face – he just got news he is being made redundant. The colleague at work who nit-picked – he feels alone and afraid. The child who was rude in the shop – she just feels unloved.

 THINGS TO DO TODAY: Imagine you are wearing your magic glasses and know that everyone has their own issues. Take nothing personally and remain tolerant and kind – everyone will benefit.

Go with the flow

As you start along a path of transformation (however small or large) beware the danger of expecting everything to be a certain way in order for you to feel like you are succeeding. Accept that life ebbs and flows and changes around you. If today is not great, can you let go of judgements about it and be OK with how it is? Struggling and resisting 'what is' does nothing more than tire you. Imagine swimming downriver to the sea – you would likely come across eddies, turbulence, waterfalls, white water channels through rocks... and of course some lovely still pools. If you struggle and go against the flow or try to fight your way back upstream you will become exhausted and probably a little battered. Let go, follow the flow and enjoy the ride.

 THINGS TO DO TODAY: What would have to happen for you to just accept how things are right now – with no illusions or denial? I wonder – could you change something by simply fully accepting it and being OK with it... for now. Take a deep breath and just be with whatever is happening. Be secure in the knowledge that nothing stays the same.

Live in the present

Treasure today – the 'now', because the fact is it is all there is. The past is a memory of another 'now' and the future is an imagined 'now'. If you were able to look back on this day how would you have liked to live it? How would you like the memory of it to be? Stop and notice things. If imagined thoughts of the future are troubling you, ask yourself 'what can I do about that right now?'. Do it – take a small step, then bring yourself back to today.

THINGS TO DO TODAY: What thoughts do you need to let go of to be fully present right now? Acknowledge them, and if there is something that requires doing about them then do it, or commit to doing it when the time is right. Then drop them and be here now.

Create a new 'you'

You can be or do whatever you wish. (OK, if you want to be a sumo wrestler and are a 5 ft diminutive woman, then a little physical realism is called for – but you could maybe try mud wrestling instead?) Many people find the concept of 'finding themselves' confusing – think instead about 'inventing' yourself. If 20 people each had a mound of play-doh and were asked to make something from it, they would all mould something different. Some may copy others but the outcomes would still be unique. And then they could all use the same pieces of play-doh to model something else, and something else. Life can be like that if you so choose. What will you make of it?

Invent yourself. Who would you like to be? Give it a go.

Enjoy the ride

How are you on journeys? Do you hurry through airports, worrying about schedules and times? Do you bury your head in a book or some work to drown out the activities around you? Do you wish it were over and you were 'there'? Do you wish you'd stayed home? On long car journeys do you feel tense and anxious about possible hold-ups? Do you dash in and out of services complaining about the costs and the service? On the train, do you plug in some headphones and avoid eye contact? Do you remember what happened the last time the train was delayed?

 THINGS TO DO TODAY: Imagine you are on a journey (you are!) and that where you are going everything is going to be just perfect. Safe in that knowledge, relax into your journey and enjoy the moment.

Life is a journey. And today is your starting point – your 'only' point!

Life is a journey. And today is your starting point – your 'only' point! How are you going to spend it? I suggest you relish it, enjoy it, pay attention to the detail, make the most of it and stop wishing it away. The exercises throughout this book are designed to help you make the most of YOU, and though some involve the use of imagination their main aim is always to allow you to feel better in the now. One day your imagined future will be your now – but don't waste today. Use the following exercise for whenever you feel like your energy is scattered and your head is in a spin. Use it to help bring you back to the present.

CALL YOUR ENERGY BACK

With practice you will be able to do this in a moment, anywhere, anytime. But first time round I suggest you sit somewhere peaceful and comfortable and take a moment to relax physically. Take a few slow, deep breaths. Close your eyes. Mentally check through all your body, relaxing each bit as you do so. With every out breath let go of more tension.

Now I want you to direct your attention into your body, I want you to feel the subtle energy field that courses through every cell of ▶

your being, feel the aliveness, the energy, the power. As you do this, become aware of where energy is 'leaking' elsewhere because of your thoughts or worries (maybe there is a stream of energy heading off towards your spouse, your children, a neighbour, a relative, work colleague. . .) and draw it back. Call back all your energy until it is 100 per cent back with you. Keep going until you are energetically completely back in your body. With a full tank of energy you are so much stronger and able to create the life you desire.

You have learned some powerful ways to change your life, through your thinking and your actions. You read this book because you wanted to change something in your life, and through your thoughts and actions you have set in motion a chain reaction of transformation. Congratulations – you have invested in you and taken a first step. I wish you all the best for every step along the way. Remember at all times: today is the first day of the rest of your life.

Appendix:
TODAY IS THE DAY YOU MAKE SURE YOU ARE READY FOR CHANGE

Are you fit and fired up for change? Would you like to regain your zest for life? Are you caring enough about yourself and feeling like you deserve the changes you desire? How you care for yourself is the foundation upon which you build your life, so if you want to make changes in any areas of your life you would benefit from making sure those foundations are as solid and secure as possible. Of course you can build on wobbly foundations – but sooner or later something will give.

Maybe the changes you desire are already based mainly on how you care for yourself – how fit and healthy (or not) you are, how nutritious your diet is and how well you rest at night. But even if they are not, and you are largely focused on work, relationships, finances, social life, your home environment, I guarantee you that looking after number one will pay dividends in every other area of your life.

Looking after number one will pay dividends

Might your health be holding you back in other areas of your life? Your love life? Work life? Social life? If you truly want to make positive life changes, make good health a priority.

Many people spend their lives feeling below par: they get by with little (and large) health niggles; manage on less than optimum energy; never experience feeling fully fit; and encounter daily stress... but vow that one day they will do something about it. And the reason they often don't is that it all just seems like too much to tackle: change diet, get fit, seek help with health issues, relax and reduce stress – NOW! But it doesn't have to be like that – you can do something about your health today. Like every other goal, you just need to start small, take a first step, then a next, and another... And the best place to start is right here with an honest assessment.

Score yourself from 1–10 against each of the following statements overleaf, where 1 equals 'this is not true at all' and 10 equals 'this is absolutely true 100 per cent of the time':

Did any of your scores surprise you? Would you like any of them to be higher? Can you imagine how life would be if your scores were all 10s? What would you need to do to nudge each score up by one point? And then one more?

The miracle of 'you'

Your body is amazing – really! It is a master of change, recreating itself continuously. I know that can be difficult to comprehend, because you probably think it looks the same most days (barring the subject of ageing, the effect of tiredness, and overindulgence and weight fluctuations), but in 21 days from today your skin will be completely new, in five months your liver will be renewed, the surface cells in your lungs regenerate every 14–21 days, your digestive tract will be renewed in four days and your bones can rebuild themselves in six weeks if broken.

Imagine for a moment that your body was a car – a car that was continually being rebuilt. A new exhaust every few weeks, a new fuel tank every couple of months, new bodywork every 21 days, all the filters changed every four days... Wow – your car would always look as good as new and drive like a dream. Or would it? What if the 'new' bits were old reconditioned bits, bits from a breaker's yard, dodgy bits, rusty parts, bits that hadn't been looked after too well beforehand? And what if the oil and fuel you used wasn't the best quality? How long would your car last?

The constant renewing of our own bodies is a great opportunity for change

The constant renewing of our own bodies is a great opportunity for change for the better, provided we ensure we use the best possible parts – and that means looking at the fuel we use to create them and how we treat them. A healthy, nutritious, balanced diet is crucial if you want to be bouncing out of bed in the morning, filled with the necessary energy and vigour to make any life changes. Whether you choose to read a book or seek the help of a qualified nutritionist, like every other desired change nothing will happen until you begin to implement the changes, so start now.

THINGS TO DO TODAY: Keep a food and drink diary for the day: write down EVERYTHING you consume – that means snacks, nibbles and sweets too! Review your list at the end of the day and remember that everything on your list has contributed to building the new you of tomorrow, next week, next month... Are you building a Ferrari or a clapped-out old banger? What could you do to ensure you pass your body's MOT?

Exercise

You don't have to spend every evening at the gym or run marathons to be fit; day-to-day activities such as walking can have equally good effects and the introduction of just 15 minutes of exercise a day can make a big difference to how you feel. Too tired? Not got enough time? Exercising can actually help with both these complaints – by boosting your vitality and mental clarity, so you can get more done more efficiently.

Experts say that walking for just half an hour five days a week is the very best way to protect your health – and you don't even have to do it all at once, 10 minutes' brisk walking three times a day will help. And it's good for your mind too: research has shown that walking for just five minutes in the countryside – especially near water – improves mental health too!

You can be imaginative and get fit with little change to your usual routine. Try doing some exercises during the adverts on TV, take a brisk brief walk at lunchtime, use your bottom stair for five minutes of step aerobics, grab a couple of tins from the kitchen cabinet and do some arm exercises while dinner is cooking... you'll soon reap the benefits and want to do more.

WOW – LOOK AT YOU!

Imagine that you've moved forward in time – a year, five years, ten years or more into the future. Imagine you are living the life of your dreams. You have made so many changes, step by small step, and you have never been healthier or happier. A health magazine has written a feature about people who turned their lives around and you are featured in it – and it includes some great pictures of you. Imagine seeing the magazine and feeling thrilled that your story can help to inspire others.

Now I am going to ask you a few questions and I want you to answer them by looking at the magazine article in your mind. Be spontaneous ▶

and quick with your answers; if you don't know an answer skip to the next question – just keep going and make it as real as possible.

What is your home like?

Who is there with you?

When did you start to turn your health around?

What was the first small step you took to increased vitality and well-being?

What do you do with your days?

What has been your best achievement?

How do you look?

How do you feel?

What advice would you give to your younger self?

How did you work through any difficult times?

What are your top three health tips?

What's in your food cupboard/fridge?

Listen-in

You live with one of your greatest gurus: your body. Your body is constantly giving you feedback and guidance about what is best for

You live with one of your greatest gurus: your body

you, but are you paying attention to what it says? Do you respond to your gut feelings? Unfortunately many people only listen to their bodies once they start to scream out in ways they cannot ignore – with pains, aches or illness. But if you learn to pay attention and listen to your body it will guide you and help you.

For example, headaches can be your body's way of te[lling]
you are not addressing its basic needs: skipping meals, not
enough water, too little sleep, insufficient exercise or stres[s.]

Every cell in the body reflects thoughts and emotions. [Have you]
ever walked into a room and had an instant sense of co[mfort or]
discomfort? This is your body giving you feedback. It ca[n tell]
you what foods are best for you and what form of exer[cise suits]
you best. Learn to listen. If you are planning changes, alw[ays check]
in with how you feel in your body about them – it won't [lie.]

 THINGS TO DO TODAY: Practise tuning-in to your bo[dy.]
your eyes and spend a few moments thinking about s[omething]
or something you feel anxious about, or something th[at worries]
you and causes stress. Feel how your body tightens a[nd your]
heart rate speeds up. Notice what happens to your s[tomach]
and your breathing.

Now spend a few moments thinking about someth[ing or]
someone that you love, or something that you find re[laxing]
and calming. Feel how your body relaxes and your br[eathing]
steadies. Notice what happens to your heart rate an[d how]
your stomach feels.

Move it!

How you use your body can also alter how you feel. [If you are]
feeling sluggish and low, you can use your body to alter [your state]
and waken yourself up. Likewise if you are feeling ene[rgised or hyped]
up you could use your body to alter your state and win[d yourself]
down. Actors use this to good effect on stage and i[n front of]
the camera. If they wish to portray someone depresse[d and low,]
they will slump their shoulders, move slowly and l[ook down]
at the ground or gaze into space. If they want to app[ear]

ABOUT THE AUTHOR

Elaine is an experienced facilitator and coach and has led workshops internationally for businesses and private individuals. Her passion is inspiring people to be the best they can be and to live the lives they truly want to lead. She lives in Somerset in the UK with her partner, son, a herd of horses and a dog.

Visit Elaine's website at **www.elaineharrison.co.uk**.

BC   8/11